The Prophetic Community

God Answers the Prayer of His Son

The Prophetic Community

God Answers the Prayer of His Son

Earl Paulk

Treasure House

An Imprint of

Destiny Image Publishers, Inc. ®

P.O. Box 310

Shippensburg, PA 17257-0310

"For where your treasure is
there will your heart be also." Matthew 6:21

ISBN 1-56043-841-X

For Worldwide Distribution
Printed in the U.S.A.

Treasure House books are available through these fine distributors outside the United States:

Christian Growth, Inc. Jalan Kilang-Timor, Singapore 0315	Vine Christian Centre Mid Glamorgan, Wales, United Kingdom
Lifestream Nottingham, England	Vision Resources Ponsonby, Auckland, New Zealand
Rhema Ministries Trading Randburg, South Africa	WA Buchanan Company Geebung, Queensland, Australia
Salvation Book Centre Petaling, Jaya, Malaysia	Word Alive Niverville, Manitoba, Canada
Successful Christian Living Capetown, Rep. of South Africa	

Inside the U.S., call toll free to order:
1-800-722-6774

Dedication

**To those who are helping to make
this Prophetic Community a reality,
my pastoral staff:**

Pastors Don and Clariece Paulk, Pete Aycock,
Barbara Benjamin, Bobby Brewer, Kirby Clements,
Michael Cole, Richard Davis, Ron Gaither, Nancy Harold,
Jim Hodgin, Ellen Housley, Robert Hunter, Chad Hyatt,
Lynn Mays, Kelly Moore, James Powers, Randy Puckett,
Bill Reily, Dan Rhodes, John Wiese, and Gino Zalunardo.

Acknowledgments

This book would not have been possible without the help of a dedicated staff who are all like family. Thank you for your undaunting love and support.

For my dear niece, LaDonna Wright, who sacrificed a part of herself to let my heart flow through this work.

For my nephew, Dana Harris, who diligently coordinated the whole project.

For the editorial staff, Wendy Long and Pat Webb, who gave themselves to organizing, compiling, and editing.

For the technical staff, Gloria Bassett, Charlotte Lemons, and Lavelle Petty, who spent many long hours in tape production and transcription.

For Renetta L. Morris, who gave of her financial sustenance to help bring this book into existence.

For the members of the Cathedral of the Holy Spirit in Atlanta, who have become not only hearers of the Word, but also doers; who seek God's presence amidst sufferings and triumphs; and who demonstrate God's power to a hostile world.

For my sweetheart, Norma, who has been a faithful wife to me and a mothering spirit for this generation.

Contents

Foreword

Bishop Earl Paulk, Jr., in this superb new book, *The Prophetic Community* challenges the Church to her biblical role in an evil society. This book needed to be written, and desperately needs to be read by church leaders throughout our world. Meticulously, Bishop Paulk defines his theological position concerning the "presentness" of the Kingdom of God, and his firm belief in the ultimate return of Christ to this planet. He describes the present role of God's Kingdom people as being a people who demonstrate His power in the midst of an "evil" world or as "Living Water" in a dry place. When Christ returns, the "glory" of His Kingdom will be demonstrated by an ultimate end to pain, sorrow, sickness, violence, and all forms of evil.

With the brilliance of a great theologian's pen, yet with the ability to make that theology understandable for the average Christian, Bishop Paulk challenges the Church to a vital role in the midst of an evil society. This book, although challenging and thought-provoking, is totally "non-confrontational." The author demonstrates such a spirit of love, compassion, and biblical logic that even the person who fanatically adheres to a dispensational eschatological view of the absence of a Kingdom presence in this dispensation, will be comfortable with his view of the role of the Church in demonstrating the "spiritual kingdom" in this age.

No spiritual leader alive today is more qualified to write this discourse on the Kingdom than my friend and brother, Bishop Earl Paulk. What qualifies him is not only his theological and philosophical understanding of the present rule and reign of Christ, but also his personal demonstration of that reign of Christ in his own life. I have had the privilege of being very close to him during a time in his life when, like his Lord, he suffered from the false accusations of those who had once seemed to be his friends. He told me time and time again that he had chosen not to defend himself, nor to attack those who falsely accused him. Instead, he simply responded as Jesus had to His accusers centuries before when He said from the cross, "Father, forgive them, for they know not what they do." It is this spirit that qualifies this great man of God to write about Christ's reign, a reign demonstrated in his personal life. Truly, for Earl Paulk, Jesus is his Lord!

Therefore, I submit this book to the Church of the latter part of this century. May we truly become the demonstration of the Kingdom's "power," and as we pray, "Come, Lord Jesus," may we look forward to that day when our King physically returns to this planet, and we witness the full manifestation of the "glory" of that Kingdom.

I believe that *The Prophetic Community* is a book whose time has come. The words of the prophet will now be heard by the Church. Like the works of the prophets who lived centuries ago, whose words were sometimes "veiled" in the "code language" of types, shadows, and symbols, there came a time when the language of the prophet was fully understood, as God unveiled those types, shadows, and symbols. The day of the unveiling of this prophet's message is upon us. May we read and understand that which the Spirit is saying to the Church.

Tommy Reid, Senior Pastor
Full Gospel Tabernacle
Buffalo, New York

Introduction

A tiny premature baby is swaddled in a cloth wrap and left on a mat near her mother. Racked with cholera and exhausted from weeks of fleeing on foot without food or clean water, the woman soon dies. The baby, still caked with blood, is placed in a cardboard box and left in a corner. Without her mother to breast-feed her, she will soon die anyway. And there are hundreds of others to be tended...

Just weeks earlier this land, overshadowed by a spectacular volcano and tucked amid banana groves and thick woodlands, was a quiet place. Once a lovely home for its people, Goma, Zaire, has now become a refuge to more than a million diseased Rwandans. The seeds of tribal hatred and civil war have reaped a harvest of starvation and death. Mutilated survivors now simply die of malnutrition and infection. Orphaned and abandoned children are everywhere. Some, fearfully emaciated, cling to the dead bodies of their parents.

"This is the beginning of the final days. This is the beginning of the Apocalypse," says one resident of Goma ("Cry the Forsaken Country," *Time*, Vol. 144, No. 5, [August 1, 1994], p. 28).

Is this truly the beginning of the last days? Is mankind on the brink of the end of the age? Is the Apocalypse real? If so, is it imminent? Jesus spoke of just such a time as this when He was here on earth. He describes to His disciples in Matthew 24 the signs that lead to His return to earth in the final days.

Now as He sat on the Mount of Olives, the disciples came to Him privately, saying, "Tell us, when will these things be? And what will be the sign of Your coming, and of the end of the age?" And Jesus answered and said to them: "Take heed that no one deceives you. For many will come in My name, saying, 'I am the Christ,' and will deceive many. And you will hear of wars and rumors of wars. See that you are not troubled; for all these things must come to pass, but the end is not yet. For nation will rise against nation, and kingdom against kingdom. And there will be famines, pestilences, and earthquakes in various places. All these are the beginning of sorrows. Then they will deliver you up to tribulation and kill you, and you will be hated by all nations for My name's sake. And then many will be offended, will betray one another, and will hate one another. Then many false prophets will rise up and deceive many. And because lawlessness will abound, the love of many will grow cold" (Matthew 24:3-12).

Jesus' description sounds dangerously close to the condition in which we find our world today:

- **Violence** rages uncontrollably in our cities.
- **Warfare** mounts in Haiti, Rwanda, Bosnia, and elsewhere.
- **Famine** spreads across the land.
- **Disease** runs rampant.
- **Betrayal** has become commonplace in business, government, and to some degree, even in the Church.

- **Lack of structure** breaks down any sense of respect for authority.

- **Rumors and allegations** in some cases give the media more power than the court systems.

- **Greed** controls the world like never before.

There is no question that our world is in grave trouble. Jesus said it would be—that it had to be—in order for God's eternal plan and divine purposes to be realized. But what about us? We call Jesus our "Savior." What kind of savior would He be to leave His children in this mess with no recourse, no plan of action, no solution?

Most people think of salvation as salvation from sins only. They think their belief in and acceptance of Jesus' gift of redemption for all mankind on the cross keeps them from going to hell and allows them to go to Heaven. They're right. But that is merely the beginning, the tip of the iceberg, of what salvation offers us. Jesus is indeed our Savior. He can save us not only from hell, but also from this chaos our world has become, if we will follow His plan.

"What is His plan?" you may ask. The prophets of old spoke of this plan:

David

*But the mercy of the Lord is from everlasting to everlasting on those who fear Him, and His righteousness to children's children, to such as keep His covenant, and to those who remember His commandments to do them. The Lord has established His throne in heaven, and **His kingdom** rules over all* (Psalm 103:17-19).

All the ends of the world shall remember and turn to the Lord, and all the families of the nations shall worship *before You. For **the kingdom** is the Lord's. And He rules over the nations* (Psalm 22:27-28).

Daniel

*And in the days of these kings the God of heaven will set up **a kingdom** which shall never be destroyed; and **the kingdom** shall not be left to other people; it shall break in pieces and consume all these kingdoms, and it shall stand forever* (Daniel 2:44).

Jesus' followers recognized it:

John the Baptist

*In those days John the Baptist came preaching in the wilderness of Judea, and saying, "Repent, for **the kingdom of heaven** is at hand!"* (Matthew 3:1-2)

Paul

*But now Christ is risen from the dead, and has become the firstfruits of those who have fallen asleep. For since by man came death, by Man also came the resurrection of the dead. For as in Adam all die, even so in Christ all shall be made alive. But each one in his own order: Christ the firstfruits, afterward those who are Christ's at His coming. Then comes the end, when He delivers **the kingdom** to God the Father, when He puts an end to all rule and all authority and power. For He must reign till He has put all enemies under His feet* (1 Corinthians 15:20-25).

*Therefore, since we are receiving **a kingdom** which cannot be shaken, let us have grace, by which we may serve God acceptably with reverence and godly fear* (Hebrews 12:28).

Peter

*For so an entrance will be supplied to you abundantly into the everlasting **kingdom** of our Lord and Savior Jesus Christ* (2 Peter 1:11).

John the Revelator

*Then the seventh angel sounded: And there were loud voices in heaven, saying, "The kingdoms of this world have become **the kingdoms of our Lord** and of His Christ, and He shall reign forever and ever!"* (Revelation 11:15)

Jesus Himself gave us the same answer:

*But seek first **the kingdom of God** and His righteousness, and all these things shall be added to you* (Matthew 6:33).

*Jesus answered and said to him, "Most assuredly, I say to you, unless one is born again, he cannot see the **kingdom of God"** * (John 3:3).

The Kingdom—God's Kingdom—is the solution, the answer, the plan. However, once we realize this, a host of questions naturally follow: What is this Kingdom? Who will run it? Who will be allowed to be in it? When and where will it be established? How do I become a part of it? No one has all the answers to these questions. Even the Bible calls the Kingdom of God a "mystery" (Mk. 4:11; Col. 1:26). But I believe that that mystery can and has been revealed to man, if only in part, by the Holy Spirit.

When Jesus took leave of this earth, He left behind a promise for all His followers—the ones alive at that time, who actually witnessed His ascension, and those of us who are His followers today.

Behold, I send the Promise of My Father upon you; but tarry in the city of Jerusalem until you are endued with power from on high (Luke 24:49).

Jesus instructed His disciples to tarry in Jerusalem after He left them until the Holy Spirit, the "Helper" whom He had promised, was sent to them. The purpose for this "Helper" is revealed in John 16:

> *But now I go away to Him who sent Me, and none of you asks Me, "Where are You going?" But because I have said these things to you, sorrow has filled your heart. Nevertheless I tell you the truth. It is to your advantage that I go away; for if I do not go away, the Helper will not come to you; but if I depart, I will send Him to you. And when He has come, He will convict the world of sin, and of righteousness, and of judgment: of sin, because they do not believe in Me; of righteousness, because I go to My Father and you see Me no more; of judgment, because the ruler of this world is judged. I still have many things to say to you, but you cannot bear them now. However, when He, the Spirit of truth, has come, He will guide you into all truth; for He will not speak on His own authority, but whatever He hears He will speak; and He will tell you things to come* (John 16:5-13).

We now know that the solution for our world's problems is the Kingdom of God. We also know that the Holy Spirit provides us with the power we need to obey the laws of this Kingdom, which is the only way we can abide in it. The Holy Spirit allows us to hear from God and to see "things to come." His power within us enables us to live in this world of greed, hatred, lust, destruction, violence, sickness, and sorrow, yet not be of it. Becoming a part of God's Kingdom is the only way to escape the desolation that surrounds us.

Remember that description—the one that so fits our world today—that Jesus gave His disciples in Matthew 24? At the end of it, Jesus again gives the solution.

But he who endures to the end shall be saved. And this gospel of the kingdom will be preached in all the world as a witness to all the nations, and then the end will come (Matthew 24:13-14).

What will happen when the end comes? Christians believe that all evil will be destroyed and Jesus will return to earth as ruler: King of kings and Lord of lords. But what will happen to those who decided not to be a part of God's Kingdom? Christians also believe that God is merciful. They also wonder if the end will come with no warning. Yet He has given us the signs in His Word; He has also given us His Holy Spirit to lead and guide us. Finally, He has given us His Kingdom. When properly demonstrated to all nations as a witness, this Kingdom will confront people with a choice. The Kingdom is God's representation of how the world ought to be. When everyone has been shown this Kingdom and been given the opportunity to enter it or reject it, then, and only then, will Jesus Christ return.

What happens after that? The glory. God's *Kingdom* will have been established as the solution for the world, and by the *power* of the Holy Spirit, people will have demonstrated how this Kingdom can and ought to work to such degree that everyone will have had the chance to accept or reject it.

When the Son of Man comes in His glory, and all the holy angels with Him, then He will sit on the throne of His glory. All the nations will be gathered before Him, and He will separate them one from another, as a shepherd divides his sheep from the goats. And He will set the sheep on His right hand, but the goats on the left. Then the King will say to those on His right hand, "Come, you blessed of My Father, inherit the kingdom prepared for you from the foundation of the world" (Matthew 25:31-34).

Now I saw a new heaven and a new earth, for the first heaven and the first earth had passed away. Also there was no more sea. Then I, John, saw the holy city, New Jerusalem, coming down out of heaven from God, prepared as a bride adorned for her husband. And I heard a loud voice from heaven saying, "Behold, the tabernacle of God is with men, and He will dwell with them, and they shall be His people. God Himself will be with them and be their God. And God will wipe away every tear from their eyes; there shall be no more death, nor sorrow, nor crying. There shall be no more pain, for the former things have passed away." Then He who sat on the throne said, "Behold, I make all things new." And He said to me, "Write, for these words are true and faithful." And He said to me, "It is done! I am the Alpha and the Omega, the Beginning and the End. I will give of the fountain of the water of life freely to him who thirsts. He who overcomes shall inherit all things, and I will be his God and he shall be My son" (Revelation 21:1-7).

No more pain, no more sorrow, no more sickness, no more of the violent devastation that is our present world. That is the *glory*. That is the end result we all dream of. It can be ours. But how do we get there? We allow the Holy Spirit to give us the power so we can demonstrate a foretaste of God's Kingdom on earth. We follow the laws of the Kingdom for as long as it takes, until all is made ready, until in the fullness of time God gives the word: It is finished! The Kingdom awaits...

Chapter 1

The Kingdom Defined

The tree of life grows in the garden of obedience.

The Kingdom of God is the spiritual realm in which God's human incarnation, Jesus Christ, is acknowledged as the King Eternal. As Head of this Kingdom, His authority is accepted and His laws are obeyed—from the heart—by people who believe on His name, who have been washed in His blood, and who have been regenerated by the Holy Spirit. Simply stated, the Kingdom of God is the place where God's authority operates.

Webster's New Universal Unabridged Dictionary defines "kingdom" as "a government or country headed by a king or queen; a monarchy, a realm, a domain" (New York: Simon & Schuster/Dorset & Baber, 1983). So what are the ingredients of a kingdom? First there must be a king. The king is the head, the one in control. Of whom is he in control? The king rules over his subjects, inhabitants of the kingdom or realm. By what does he control or govern them? He uses laws. Thus the Kingdom of God is like any other kingdom in its structure. It has a king (Jesus) who rules His subjects (Christians) through a set of laws.

God's Kingdom has total order, an order expressed in individuals and in society corporately. Entrance into this Kingdom is through the personal new birth. The overall character of the Kingdom is seen in the character of Jesus. This Kingdom demands total obedience, but brings total freedom. The time of its culmination is known by God alone. Its ultimate goal is to replace the present world order (see Rev. 11:15). This Kingdom comes to earth through a gradual process until earth again has the same rule as Heaven.

Why do I say, "until earth *again* has the same rule as Heaven"? The earth at one time possessed a portion of the total order and rule of Heaven. This was in the Garden of Eden, the place where God's purpose for the earth was begun. God's original plan was to create and maintain a universal community where creativity and productivity could flourish in an environment of health, peace, and harmony.

The Garden of Eden was God's Kingdom here on earth. He was the King. He had subjects—His creation, Adam and Eve— and He gave them laws to live by. One of these laws said they were forbidden to eat of the tree of the knowledge of good and evil. Unfortunately, Adam and Eve broke that law. They were able to break the law because God had given them the power of choice when He created them in His image. Out of this power and freedom of choice man chose to be his own god, to rule himself, by disregarding a law God had given him. Perhaps Adam and Eve thought they were smarter than God in finding another way to live in His Kingdom without obeying His laws. They were wrong. As I stated earlier, this Kingdom demands total obedience. Thus they were banished from the Garden. God's plan had seemingly failed when man disobeyed. But He did not give up on it. He simply revealed a bigger and better plan to overcome man's failure.

That plan was Jesus. Because of Adam and Eve's disobedience, all of mankind after them was born into a sinful, fallen world. However, God sent His own Son to redeem mankind back to Himself, and to give man another chance for God's Kingdom to work on earth again under the reign of His Son, the King.

The entire Bible is a record of this plan—of God redeeming mankind and reestablishing His order. At this point you may be asking, "What is so important about God's order? Where did it come from? Why is mankind obligated to follow it?" Whether or not people buy into the idea of God's Kingdom depends totally upon their belief in God—a supreme, all-knowing, all-powerful being who holds all authority in earth and in Heaven. Like Adam, we are all created in God's image; therefore, we have the power of choice. It is every person's prerogative not to believe in God. That's how He made us—He made us to choose. But, if you are like me and like so many others, knowing deep inside that this intricate universe did not appear from nowhere, then you believe in God. When you look at the order and design of nature, of the animal kingdom, of the human body—how can you deny that somewhere there is a Creator whose wisdom and power are infinite? The first fundamental of the Kingdom of God is just this—belief in God and in His total authority in the universe.

The God of the Universe

To learn about the Kingdom then, we must learn about God. God is a God of order and design, a God of pattern. He often works in the same ways. He is the ultimate teacher, patiently repeating things over and over for us so we can learn. In fact, a pattern existed in what happened in the Garden of Eden. Did you know that that was not the first time God encountered rebellion against His order? The incident in the Garden was very much like another that took place in Heaven.

Long before God created man, He created angels who worshiped Him in the heavens. There were three archangels or ruling angels named Michael, Gabriel, and Lucifer. Lucifer was a very beautiful angel in charge of worship (see Ezek. 28:12-15). Lucifer knew he was beautiful. He knew he was talented. He also was ambitious. It is recorded in Isaiah that Lucifer said in his heart:

... "I will ascend into heaven, I will exalt my throne above the stars of God; I will also sit on the mount of the congregation on the farthest sides of the north; I will ascend above the heights of the clouds, I will be like the Most High" (Isaiah 14:13-14).

A battle ensued between the angels, some joining Lucifer and others joining Michael. Michael, along with those loyal to God, prevailed, and Lucifer and the other rebellious angels were expelled from Heaven and cast down to earth. Lucifer became known as satan, and he reigned on earth until....

Have you ever wondered what happened between verse 1 and verse 2 of Genesis 1?

In the beginning God created the heavens and the earth (Genesis 1:1).

The earth was without form, and void; and darkness was on the face of the deep. And the Spirit of God was hovering over the face of the waters (Genesis 1:2).

Why would a God of order and design create anything that was without form and void? It would have been against God's nature to create anything chaotic. So how did it come to be in that shape—formless, void, and dark? I believe a great span of time passed between verses 1 and 2 of Genesis chapter 1. I believe that's where lucifer, now satan, and his cohorts were thrown when they were cast out of Heaven. Their rebellious spirits created the confusion and darkness that was on the earth until God decided to establish His order again through the Garden of Eden, and Adam and Eve. That was the whole reason for the Garden! After lucifer's fall, the earth became a battleground between order and chaos. Anarchy, rebellion, and lawlessness reigned on the earth because of satan's presence. God created man in His image to confront the evil of satan on earth and reclaim it for God's Kingdom by correcting the rebellious spirit there. Sadly, man failed. But God, the ultimate teacher, kept working with man. Out of the fall came the promise that through the seed of the woman would come the final victory.

Jesus is that seed. He was born into this world, a descendant of Adam and Eve—very flesh, yet very God. All human frailty and weakness resided in Him. In Him also, however, was divinity, the possibility of living a sinless life. He who knew no sin was made sin for us, for all mankind (see 2 Cor. 5:21). He lived out His life in total obedience to God. He never wavered from His purpose. So God granted Him all authority in Heaven and in earth (see Mt. 28:18). Jesus walked the same earth as Adam—but where Adam failed, Jesus was victorious (see 1 Cor. 15:21-22). Because of this victory, Jehovah God—omnipotent, omniscient, omnipresent; from whom all power and authority originates—granted that Jesus, His Son, would be King of His Kingdom.

The King Eternal

The second fundamental of the Kingdom is this: Jesus is the King Eternal. He is the fulfillment of the law and the prophets (see Mt. 5:17). In Him dwells all the fullness of the Godhead (see Col. 2:9). God came to earth as a man and gave us hope that rebellion could be overcome. The first Adam failed in disobedience, but the second Adam, Jesus, was victorious through obedience.

Obedience is an integral part of God's Kingdom. It is what made it possible for Jesus to become the King.

So many people know Jesus as their Savior and Redeemer. He is our Savior and Redeemer, of course. But to truly understand the Kingdom of God, we also must know Jesus as King. If we miss the kingship of Jesus, we miss the whole message of God's Kingdom. He is the One to whom we must bow. Every kingdom of this world will in the end subject itself to the Kingdom of the King Eternal, Jesus Christ.

One of the principles found in the Word of God states that to be in a position of authority, one must be under authority. An account in Matthew illustrates this principle.

Now when Jesus had entered Capernaum, a centurion came to Him, pleading with Him, saying, "Lord, my servant is lying at home paralyzed, dreadfully tormented." And Jesus said to him, "I will come and heal him." The centurion answered and said, "Lord, I am not worthy that You should come under my roof. But only speak a word, and my servant will be healed. For I also am a man under authority, having soldiers under me. And I say to this one, 'Go,' and he goes; and to another, 'Come,' and he comes; and to my servant, 'Do this,' and he does it." When Jesus heard it, He marveled, and said to those who followed, "Assuredly, I say to you, I have not found such great faith, not even in Israel!" (Matthew 8:5-10)

The centurion was a military man in charge of many soldiers. He understood the principle of speaking a command and knowing it would be followed even if he was not there to see that it was. He understood authority. He knew the chain of command. However, he had not become a man of great power and authority the first day he joined the army. He probably started as military men still do today—as "grunts" who must obey even the smallest command of their superior officers. Little by little, as the Roman army found him obedient and faithful, he was promoted to a position of power. But it was all because he understood authority. He had been on the bottom end of it and worked his way up. He earned the right to be in authority.

In our case, God put man on the earth to subdue it and take dominion over it (see Gen. 1:28). But we can't give orders until we have learned to take them. We can't be in that position of power and authority until we have been under authority. Under whose authority do we serve? The authority belongs to the One who earned it—the Eternal King of the Kingdom, Jesus.

Subjects of the Kingdom

The third fundamental of the Kingdom is its subjects. The subjects of the Kingdom are those who willingly come under the Lordship of Christ and obey Him from the heart (see Rom. 6:17). Much of the obedience of God's people in the Old Testament was a result of fear. They obeyed God's laws because the consequences of disobeying those laws were severe. When Jesus came, though, He wrote the laws of God on the people's hearts. Then people obeyed because they wanted to, because they loved the King who gave the laws.

How do we become subjects of the Kingdom of God? A man named Nicodemus asked Jesus this question. Jesus answered him by saying, "You must be born again" (see Jn. 3:1-3). This obviously does not mean a natural birth, but a spiritual birth into a new way of thinking, into obeying new laws, and into serving a new King.

Once we become subjects, we must become obedient. Before Jesus left the earth, He gave His subjects a command. We, as His subjects today, are still responsible to obey this command. "And

He said to them, 'Go into all the world and preach the gospel to every creature' " (Mk. 16:15). When Jesus was here, He was the light of the world (see Jn. 9:5). Now that He is gone, that light—His light—shines through us, His subjects. We become that influence for good upon planet Earth that He was while He was here.

Along with being light, we also are asked to be salt (see Mt. 5:13-14). The purpose of salt is to flavor, to season, and to preserve. We are to preserve God's laws here on earth. We must move into the dark places and bring His light. We must change society. We must become the reflection of the Light of the world, the King Eternal. We must influence for the positive every other kingdom we come in contact with.

Subjects are warned in Matthew 5:13 not to lose their flavor, or savor. What does that mean? It means we are not to become ineffective, but to remain pure so we can do our job in the world. We must realize that the Kingdom of God is birthed in confrontation. At the time of Jesus' birth, the Jewish people were a nation oppressed under the Roman empire. Jesus Himself confronted many—the moneychangers in the temple, the men trying to stone the adulterous woman, the rich young ruler, and even demonic spirits. After His death, the disciples were faced with ridicule and disbelief. Members of the early Church were persecuted beyond belief; they were mocked, tortured, and hideously killed to provide sporting entertainment for the Romans.

When the Kingdom of God meets the kingdom or system of this world, it produces friction. Perhaps that is what this Scripture means: "...the kingdom of heaven suffers violence, and the violent take it by force" (Mt 11:12). Is it a physical violence? Probably not. We must be "violent" in our convictions, "violent" in our efforts to stop the forces of darkness in our world—righteously indignant at injustices we observe. God's subjects must violently, passionately, and vehemently work to establish His Kingdom.

How do we properly handle all this friction, violence, and confrontation without getting "burned out"? Without losing our savor as salt and becoming ineffective? Without becoming religious bigots who fall into the trap of intolerance and judgmentalism? It is a mystery of the Kingdom that in the midst of turmoil, violence, and confrontation, there is peace. That peace comes when His subjects are in His will, doing the work He has instructed them to do.

Jesus is our peace. He is called the Prince of Peace (see Is. 9:6). Angels heralded His birth with the now familiar saying, "Peace on earth, good will toward men" (see Lk. 2:14). Peace is a fruit of the Holy Spirit (see Gal. 5:22). David proclaims in the Psalms, "Great peace have those who love Your [God's] law" (Ps. 119:165a). Perfect peace is promised to those who keep their mind stayed on God (see Is. 26:3). Finally, Jesus comforts His followers with these words:

*But the Helper, the Holy Spirit, whom the Father will send in My name, He will teach you all things, and bring to your remembrance all things that I said to you. **Peace** I leave with you, My **peace** I give to you; not as the world gives do I give to you. Let not your heart be troubled, neither let it be afraid* (John 14:26-27).

*These things I have spoken to you, that in Me you may have **peace**. In the world you will have tribulation; but be of good cheer, I have overcome the world* (John 16:33).

Even though tribulation is promised, so is God's peace. It is a peace that passes all understanding because it comes in the midst of turbulent and violent surroundings (see Phil. 4:7).

"What about Matthew 10:34," you might ask, "where Jesus says He did not come to bring peace, but a sword?" A common term for a police officer or someone in law enforcement is a "peace officer." Yet do you think of these public servants as people who go around all the time being nice to people? I'm sure they are sometimes, but most of the time they are surrounded by violent circumstances. They are constantly in the midst of conflict and confrontation because one of their responsibilities is to "keep" the peace. How do they do this? It is sometimes done violently. They carry "swords," as Jesus referred to them, or "guns," as we would refer to them today. But their "swords" or weapons bring peace because they keep order. So it was with Jesus and still is today with the subjects of His Kingdom. There can be peace on earth only when we preserve it by following the laws of the Kingdom. Thus there is a paradox: Because we are violent in our hearts against darkness, there is peace.

The Kingdom Laws

The fourth fundamental of the Kingdom is its laws. What immediately comes to your mind when you think about "God's laws"? Most of us probably think first of the Ten Commandments, which God gave to His people through Moses in the Old Testament (see Ex. 20). That's a good place to start. Obeying these laws concerning stealing, killing, lying, committing adultery, taking the Lord's name in vain, worshiping God alone, making graven images, coveting, keeping the Sabbath holy and honoring your father and mother are the foundation of the Christian life. But when Jesus came, He expanded these laws. You still keep these commandments, but to enter the Kingdom, you are asked to go a step further.

The laws of the Kingdom are a matter of the heart. Have you ever heard of someone "sitting down on the outside, but standing up on the inside"? That means you sit down as you're told, but in your heart, you are defiant. You have obeyed the law because you had to and not because you wanted to. In the Old Testament, under the Ten Commandments, all a person had to do was obey the laws outwardly. Jesus, though, wants the subjects of His Kingdom to be obedient inwardly as well.

> *Now behold, one came and said to Him, "Good Teacher, what good thing shall I do that I may have eternal life?" So He said to him, "Why do you call Me good? No one is good but One, that is, God. But if you want to enter into life, keep the commandments." He said to Him, "Which ones?" Jesus said, " 'You shall not murder,' 'You shall not commit adultery,' 'You shall not steal,' 'You shall not bear false witness,' 'Honor your father and your mother,' and, 'You shall love your neighbor as yourself.' " The young man said to Him, "All these things I have kept from my youth. What do I still lack?" Jesus said to him, "If you want to be perfect, go, sell what you have and give to the poor, and you will have treasure in heaven; and come, follow Me." But when the young man heard that saying, he went away sorrowful, for he had great possessions* (Matthew 19:16-22).

Jesus used this experience with the rich young ruler to teach His disciples about the Kingdom. He told them that it is hard for a rich man to enter into the Kingdom; it is actually easier for a camel to go through the eye of a needle than for a rich man to give up his possessions and seek the Kingdom of God first (see Mt. 19:23-24).

We know from the Bible that Jesus gave two commandments that are the core of the ten already established. In Matthew 22 the Pharisees were asking Him questions, trying to get Him to contradict Himself or "slip up" in some way. When they asked Him what the greatest commandment was, He answered them:

> ... " 'You shall love the Lord your God with all your heart, with all your soul, and with all your mind.' This is the first and great commandment. And the second is like it: 'You

shall love your neighbor as yourself.' On these two commandments hang all the Law and the Prophets" (Matthew 22:37-40).

Jesus always brought things back to the motive of the heart. It doesn't matter what is on paper; what matters is the attitude with which we do things. Jesus told His followers to do as He did. He is our ultimate example. If we have the character of Jesus, then we have the character of the Kingdom. We will live out what is right if we live as He did. Most people, however, want things "on paper." So Jesus even gave us that too.

Jesus' Sermon on the Mount is recorded in Matthew, chapters 5, 6, and 7. I will not take the space to reprint it in its entirety here. I will only highlight it, but the Sermon on the Mount contains information that we, as subjects of the Kingdom, need to read for ourselves. We need to not only read it, but also study it, absorb it, and get it into our hearts and spirits. It is the bulk of the laws of the Kingdom.

He began with the Beatitudes:

Blessed are the poor in spirit,
    For theirs is the kingdom of heaven.
Blessed are those who mourn,
    For they shall be comforted.
Blessed are the meek,
    For they shall inherit the earth.
Blessed are those who hunger and thirst for righteousness,
    For they shall be filled.
Blessed are the merciful,
    For they shall obtain mercy.
Blessed are the pure in heart,
    For they shall see God.
Blessed are the peacemakers,

For they shall be called the sons of God.
Blessed are those who are persecuted for righteousness' sake,
For theirs is the kingdom of heaven.

Matthew 5:3-10

Jesus sets the tone here for following the laws of the Kingdom from the heart. After assuring the people that He did not come to destroy or change the law they had already been given, He asked them to go that step further.

You have heard that it was said to those of old, "You shall not murder, and whoever murders will be in danger of the judgment." But I say to you that whoever is angry with his brother without a cause shall be in danger of the judgment. And whoever says to his brother, "Raca!" shall be in danger of the council. But whoever says, "You fool!" shall be in danger of hell fire. ... You have heard that it was said to those of old, "You shall not commit adultery." But I say to you that whoever looks at a woman to lust for her has already committed adultery with her in his heart (Matthew 5:21-22,27-28).

He goes on through chapter 7 of Matthew to address everything from marriage and divorce to fasting and judging people. Always He begins with the law the people already know and then asks them to go a step further, to make it a matter of heart and not simply one of conduct. This is the heart and core of the laws of the Kingdom. Then, toward the end of the sermon, Jesus gives a warning:

Enter by the narrow gate; for wide is the gate and broad is the way that leads to destruction, and there are many who go in by it. Because narrow is the gate and difficult is the way which leads to life, and there are few who find it (Matthew 7:13-14).

You might think this is a discouraging passage, but it is rather realistic. Obeying laws such as "love your enemies"; "do good to those who despitefully use you"; "if your neighbor slaps you on one cheek, turn the other one to him"; and "go the second mile" is no easy task. This is why Jesus said there are "few" who find this way, this Kingdom way of life. Nevertheless, we are not without help. Jesus sent us the Holy Spirit to be our Helper and our Guide. He also left for us His own life as an example. Thus to truly obey all the laws of the Kingdom, we must take on the character of Jesus. We must always and in all things strive to be like Him.

Chapter 2

The Kingdom Expressed

The Kingdom of God does not come
by observation, but by demonstration.

We have established that the Kingdom of God is the realm where the all-powerful Creator, God, has given to His Son, Jesus, the King Eternal, the authority to be King and to rule the subjects of the Kingdom, the subjects being those who willingly enter the Kingdom and obey its laws from their hearts. We also know that we enter this Kingdom by a personal new birth, or salvation. That is its structure. The next questions that arise ask: What are the purposes of the Kingdom? How do we as its subjects express it or incorporate it into our daily lives?

Even more basic is this question: Why is the Kingdom of God even necessary? The obvious reason is that it is the ultimate and final solution for our world. It is the means by which God redeems mankind to Himself. But there are also some more specific purposes for the Kingdom of God.

The Four Purposes of the Kingdom

The first purpose of the Kingdom is to maintain order in the universe. We already know that God originally created the universe to be ordered and structured. That order was challenged by lucifer and his cohorts when they rebelled. When they were cast to earth, they confused the order that existed here. God then began to reestablish His order in the Garden of Eden through man, Adam and Eve. When they too rebelled, God sent His Son, Himself incarnate, to again reestablish His order.

We, as humans, do not "establish" the Kingdom. The Kingdom, God's order, has existed from the beginning of time. It is as eternal and infinite as God is. Even though it was challenged and confused by the rebellion of angels and men, God's order has never been destroyed. It still exists, however clouded and hidden it has become in our present society. So as His subjects, it is our job to maintain God's original order, even if it is in small communities as examples to the rest of the world.

The second purpose of the Kingdom is to make God's presence known or felt among His creation. The Church at large is to play a specific role in demonstrating the Kingdom of God to this world which has, for the most part, forgotten God's order. Jesus was called "Emmanuel," meaning "God with us." Just as Jesus brought the presence of God among men in His day, so must we today as subjects of the Kingdom bring His presence into our world.

The third purpose of the Kingdom is to provide man with a choice, or an opportunity, to "plug in" to God's order. It is our responsibility as subjects to introduce this Kingdom to others and urge them to enter in and become actively involved with God in battling the evil forces of rebellion that disrupted His order. We battle these forces by replacing rebellion with obedience, first as individuals, then as a larger group, the Church—God's representation of the Kingdom.

The fourth purpose of the Kingdom is to constantly assure all of creation—including evil principalities and powers—that the Kingdom of God will be victorious in the end. Revelation 11:15 tells us that every other kingdom of this earth shall finally become a part of the Kingdom of God. Every other force will be put down. Even satan himself will be bound and done away with. His authority will be stripped from him and God's Kingdom will be the only one "left standing," with no other challengers left. The Kingdom is the unchallenged rule of God through Christ.

The purposes of the Kingdom of God, then, are to maintain order, to make God's presence known and felt among His creation, to give man an opportunity to be birthed into the Kingdom and join God's battle to regain His order on earth, and to assure us that God is always at work overcoming every other kingdom that challenges His.

United for the Kingdom

Before you sell your houses and lands and hit the road in search of "The Kingdom," let me inform you that it does not exist as an earthly kingdom in one geographical location. There is no "mecca" to which you must make a pilgrimage. The Kingdom of God is in the heart. It is your heart God is after. That is the place where He does His work. Once you understand that the Kingdom is in your heart, and you follow its laws as a part of your daily life, then the Kingdom exists wherever you are. You may be wondering, "But how can one single person be an example of this huge Kingdom and take on the responsibility of fighting evil?" Subjects of the Kingdom need to find each other and work together. There is strength in numbers.

God started establishing the Kingdom with the early Church, a community of Kingdom subjects who all understood their mission in this world and worked together to accomplish it. Somewhere along the way, though, this structure that had been set up, the Church, became fragmented and separated. Different classifications (today we call them denominations) of the group emerged, all emphasizing different facets of the Kingdom. This "division" would have been fine had the people recognized that each subgroup had only a facet or two and that they needed each other to represent the total Kingdom. Instead, the subgroups ended up warring against each other and claiming they each had the complete truth all to themselves. They got so caught up in their feuding that Paul chided them for it in First Corinthians 1:10-15. They became exclusive and started making up rules and regulations that Jesus never intended.

One fundamental principle of the Kingdom is that we shouldn't stand in judgment of others who preach that the Lord Jesus Christ is King. Even though we will not all totally agree in doctrine or method, we should agree that Jesus is the King of the Kingdom and that all His laws must be obeyed. We can all have different areas of emphasis. That's fine. But in our hearts we must be unified. Our goal of reestablishing God's order is the same. We may all go about it in different ways, but the end result is what we hold in common. Presently we cannot reach our goal because we are still at war. We are still so insecure that we feel we cannot trust others to have the "true" Kingdom message if they baptize a different way or receive members into the church in a different manner than we do.

Unfortunately the fragmentation of the Church that began soon after its inception continues today. Just think, if Jesus were to return today for His Bride, as the Bible describes the Church, He would be rather torn. Who would be the Bride? The Catholics?

The Protestants? The Pentecostals? The Presbyterians? The Baptists? He will not choose. There must be one Bride, the Church Eternal, united.

Just as Eve was a suitable helpmeet to Adam, so the Church must become a suitable Bride for Jesus. We've got to grow up and stop fighting each other. We've got to stop thinking that our little group of 250 people who meet together weekly, sing the same songs, and believe the same doctrines are the only ones Jesus will return for. Each community or local church that follows Kingdom laws and principles must understand that they are only a small part of a larger group—the Bride of Christ, the Church at large. Matthew 24:14 says that Jesus will return (the end will come) when the gospel of the Kingdom has been preached and demonstrated to all the earth. How can one little group do that all by itself? It can't! That's why we've got to start relying on each other. Some who have the Kingdom message will be in Brazil and they will be responsible for that area. Others will be in the United States; others in Europe, in Asia, and in Africa. Eventually there will be a mature Church whose counterparts recognize each other because they follow the same laws and are under the rule of the same King, Jesus. When that maturity is complete and we become that living witness, then the King of Glory can come again. We will have finally become the answer to Jesus' prayer in John 17:20-21.

I do not pray for these alone, but also for those who will believe in Me through their word; that they all may be one, as You, Father, are in Me, and I in You; that they also may be one in Us, that the world may believe that You sent Me (John 17:20-21).

Exemplifying the Kingdom

Each local church should be a microcosmic example of the Kingdom of God for all the people in their geographical area. How else will they know the Kingdom even exists, or that there is a possibility for change in the present world order? In order to become such an example, each church must be properly structured. After all, how can we tell the world not to judge when we judge them and each other? How can we tell them that their goal should be to live in peace when we cannot live in peace with other churches or even with those in our own church? How can we tell them that God is the ultimate authority and that the pastor in each church is the representative of that authority when a committee can vote the pastor in or out as they please? God so wants His Church, the representation of His Kingdom of order and peace, to be an example for the world to look upon and realize the possibility of living another way.

At this point in history the Kingdom of God still functions through His Church in spite of its frailty. The Church is God's means of showing satan that the principles and laws of the Kingdom do indeed work—and that obedience will overcome rebellion in the end. The very heart and core of the Kingdom is learning the character of God, which was lived out through Jesus, through the truths He taught and the way He handled situations. He is our example. Thus we must become subject to Jesus as Lord and King. We subject ourselves to Him in such a way that it becomes a witness or example to the world. Through our subjection we overcome the powers of this world and prepare ourselves for the return of the Lord Jesus Christ.

That is the process. But the process has been hampered by the divisive forces still present in God's Church. Jesus cannot return for His Bride yet because there is no unity within her. We are like little children running around with our little piece of the puzzle and thinking we have the whole thing. We shout, "Repent, for the Kingdom of God is at hand! Jesus is coming! Get ready!" What a joke!

The world pays no more attention to us than the animals did to the fictional character "Chicken Little" in that famous children's story, as she ran around screaming, "The sky is falling! The sky is falling!" When will the world pay attention to us? They will take notice when we are able to show them a better way. They will listen to us when we have proven that the solutions we offer them really work for us and can work for them too. They will listen to us when they see us doing a better job than the government at educating children, taking care of the little ones and the elderly, feeding and clothing the poor, comforting the sick, and bringing peace to our violent, crime-ridden streets.

The Pattern of Show and Tell

Jesus established a pattern for teaching His disciples when He lived here on earth. Luke writes in the Acts of the Apostles, "The former account I made...of all that Jesus began both to do and teach" (Acts 1:1). Jesus did and then He taught. This occurs over and over throughout the Gospels. I mentioned in the previous chapter the Sermon on the Mount from the Gospel of Matthew, which I believe contains the bulk of the laws of the Kingdom. When Jesus preached this sermon, did He just go up on a mountain and begin talking to the air and somehow, mysteriously, people gathered to listen to Him? No! He got a crowd together first. How did He do that? We find the answer at the end of Matthew 4.

And Jesus went about all Galilee, teaching in their synagogues, preaching the gospel of the kingdom, and healing all kinds of sickness and all kinds of disease among the people. Then His fame went throughout all Syria; and they brought to Him all sick people who were afflicted with various diseases and torments, and those who were demonpossessed, epileptics, and paralytics; and He healed them. Great multitudes followed Him—from Galilee, and from

Decapolis, Jerusalem, Judea, and beyond the Jordan (Matthew 4:23-25).

So ends chapter 4, and the very next chapter begins the Sermon on the Mount. This shows that Jesus did first, then taught. He performed miracles. He healed their sick. In short, He got their attention first. He offered them a solution that they could see for themselves would work—and then He sat them down and taught them. He told them why it would work. He taught them that they could have miracles and healings like that all the time if they would become a part of His Kingdom.

I like to call this concept "demonstration and communication." You may have the best idea in the whole world. You may have the cure for cancer, a more efficient way to fuel an automobile, or the design for a mechanism to make some difficult task easier—but if you never communicate it to anybody or don't even have the tools to communicate it with, then what good does your idea do for people? So you know about the Kingdom of God. So you know it is the solution to the world's problems. What good is that information doing the world if you never share it? More importantly, what good is that information doing anybody if you allow it to remain just that—information? We've got to live it out—demonstrate it! We've got to show the world it works. We live in a skeptical, cynical world full of people who have an attitude of "I'll believe it when I see it." How do we make them see it?

We make the world see it by showing them a better way, just as Jesus did. The Kingdom of God is about excellence. We must do the very best we can with whatever we have. Perhaps God has given you a talent to sing. Many performers began their singing "careers" in their church. Then when people realized how good they were, record contracts began to materialize. Agents showed up and soon their gift was no longer used to glorify the One who gave it to them. This happens all too often. What happens? God is the Creator of everything that is good. He created music, dance, drama, art—everything! Satan, though, created nothing. He has no ability to create. But he does use whatever people will allow him to use.

Somewhere along the way, the Church became convinced that certain things were "of God" and certain things were "of the devil." Someone decided that dance was not a mode through which we could praise God. Someone decided that drama was not "of God." So a void was created for these arts. Guess who picked them up and put them to use? That's right, satan. Remember, he used to be in charge of worship in Heaven. He was musical. He was dramatic. When the Church abandoned these God-created arts, he was right there, ready to snatch back a part of himself that had been lost. Thus he uses these things to further his own kingdom.

One reason the Kingdom of God does not appeal to more people than it does is that the Church has become a place of "don'ts." All people see of the Church is the long list of things they must give up and no longer enjoy. I say that's ridiculous! It's time we bring all things back under the submission of God's Kingdom and use them properly to worship our Creator. But the world will never see anything the Church does if the Church is no better than what they have in the world. That's why we must demonstrate excellence. We must present the world with something they cannot find anywhere else. Then they will come and see. When they ask, "Where did you get such marvelous music, and who trained you to sing and dance so well?" we will answer, "God. God gave us this talent and these wonderful ideas. He gave us the ability to perform the way that we do." They will want to know more and more. In this way we have the perfect opportunity to introduce them to the Kingdom. We demonstrate, then communicate; we do and teach—just like Jesus.

Chapter 3

The Kingdom Delegated

**Matters of morality can never
be legislated by civil government.**

*There is one body and one Spirit, just as you were called in
one hope of your calling; one Lord, one faith, one baptism;
one God and Father of all, who is above all, and through
all, and in you all. But to each one of us grace was given
according to the measure of Christ's gift. Therefore He
says, "When He ascended on high, He led captivity captive, and gave gifts to men." ... And He Himself gave some
to be apostles, some prophets, some evangelists, and some
pastors and teachers, for the equipping of the saints for the
work of ministry, for the edifying of the body of Christ, till
we all come to the unity of the faith and of the knowledge of
the Son of God, to a perfect man, to the measure of the stat-
ure of the fullness of Christ; that we should no longer be
children, tossed to and fro and carried about with every
wind of doctrine, by the trickery of men, in the cunning*

craftiness of deceitful plotting, but, speaking the truth in love, may grow up in all things into Him who is the head— Christ—from whom the whole body, joined and knit together by what every joint supplies, according to the effective working by which every part does its share, causes growth of the body for the edifying of itself in love (Ephesians 4:4-8,11-16).

God is supreme. We know that all power and authority rest in Him—from the beginning of time. At various times He has chosen to delegate or assign His authority. For instance, He invested Jesus, His Son, with His authority to be King of the Kingdom. As we have just read in this Scripture from Ephesians, Jesus likewise invested His Church with this authority when He ascended to the Father. It's a very simple progression: God gave Jesus authority when He came to earth, and when Jesus left this earth, He passed that authority on to the Church. Why? We need God's authority to do our work on earth, just as Jesus did. We need His power to complete the task He asked us to do before He left—to preach the gospel of His Kingdom to the whole earth.

This passage in Ephesians is so key to understanding the Kingdom. It summarizes virtually everything I discussed in the previous chapter. Everyone who follows the laws of the Kingdom is a part of God's Church, His Body, His Kingdom. Yet each of us has different functions, different gifts, and different emphases. We then are responsible for doing the part that is our share, as well as for recognizing that others have gifts and callings also. We must allow them to do their share. We must recognize that our brothers and sisters are also part of Christ's Body and rely on them to do the parts of God's assignment that we cannot do. When all the parts of God's Kingdom recognize each other and begin to work together for the common goal, without jealousy and insecurity, then we have become the mature Bride. We are connected as a human body is: "...joined and knit together by what every joint supplies, according to the effective working by which every part does its share..." (Eph. 4:16).

The Church as a Body

The Church represents Christ on earth today. After all, that is why it is called "the Body of Christ." Like a body, as we have learned, the Church has many members or parts. They are in different geographical locations, using different methods, and possessing different gifts, but all follow the laws of the Kingdom with the common goal of reestablishing God's order in the world.

> But now indeed there are many members, yet one body. And the eye cannot say to the hand, "I have no need of you"; nor again the head to the feet, "I have no need of you." ... And if one member suffers, all the members suffer with it; or if one member is honored, all the members rejoice with it. Now you are the body of Christ, and members individually (1 Corinthians 12:20-21,26-27).

The Body of Christ is also much like a corporation or business. It has different branches that accomplish different things and serve different purposes, yet all work for the same president to accomplish a common goal. Also, just as a company president assigns different tasks to different people within his organization, so does Jesus in His Kingdom. We call this "delegating authority." Jesus gives different people different assignments in order to accomplish the goal of reestablishing His order here on earth.

This principle of delegated authority is a part of the Kingdom concept. All positions of authority that exist in the world then, if properly understood, are actually assignments from God and are based in His supreme authority. We would expect the Church to be part of God's delegated authority, yet there are other areas as well that are just as godly. In the grand scheme of things, these other authority positions carry just as much importance as the Church does in God's Kingdom. We simply don't normally think of them as "spiritual." For example, the family structure is part of God's delegated authority to maintain His order here on earth. The civil government also is part of it, as are schools.

Parental Authority

However, let's talk about the family. The family unit is God's idea. He created Adam and Eve, made them interdependent, and gave them the ability to reproduce themselves. This act of reproduction was not over the minute the baby was delivered, however. Adam and Eve then were given the responsibility of raising that child until he could function on his own in the world. This first family unit provides the model for the rest of mankind. Parents are put in a position of authority by God and are responsible for seeing that their offspring reach adulthood.

As we continue, you will find that there are two words that always go together: authority and responsibility. When God gives you authority, it is not to be abused or mishandled, for with authority always comes responsibility. If you fail to use your authority responsibly, then you lose it.

What are the responsibilities of parents? The first is to provide security for their household physically, financially, emotionally, and spiritually. When a baby is born, the infant is totally and completely helpless. A newborn cannot care for himself in any way. The baby will die if his parents don't see that he is fed. As the child grows he learns. He learns to walk, to speak, to feed himself with a spoon. But the responsibility of a parent doesn't end here either. Even when a child can physically feed and dress himself, he still has no ability to obtain the food or clothes in order to do so. That's what parents are for.

Many parents fulfill the responsibilities of providing for their children financially and physically, but they completely neglect the emotional and spiritual security of their children. The same parent who wouldn't dream of letting his child go physically hungry may fail to ask, when he picks up the child from school, "Did you have a good day? What did you learn?" A child also hungers for attention, to know that his parents are concerned with every aspect of his life. He wants his parents to know what is important to him and what hurts his feelings, not just care about whether he is fed and clothed. Those other needs are just as basic to him.

Children, especially those in the first all-important formative years of their lives, learn only what we as parents teach them. I doubt that any parent has experienced her three-year-old or four-year-old coming to her with his health concerns and asking to be taken to the doctor to receive immunization, or for a toothbrush so he can begin good oral hygiene. Children brush their teeth because their parents teach them to. They receive appropriate health care because their parents see to it that they get it.

I am always amazed to hear the testimonies of some people who say, "I never heard about Jesus until someone at work told me." Where were the parents? Many times, if asked, these parents would answer, "Well, it never came up. My children never asked me about God." Their children probably never asked to go to school either, but at the age of six they were dropped off in front of a brick building and told to go and listen and do as they were told. How can children be expected to know God exists if parents don't tell them? How can they be expected to know the difference between right and wrong without their parents' aid? Just as a child's physical safety and emotional well-being are a parent's responsibility, so is his spiritual life. It is the parents' job to teach their children about God and to put into them the values the parents want them to have. It doesn't just "happen." Security in every area is the parents' first responsibility.

The second responsibility of parents is to counsel and give direction to their children. As I said before, children know only what they are taught. It is easy to control what they are taught or what they learn when they are small because then the parents have total control over the children's environment. But the older they get, the more people and places they are exposed to. Children constantly hear and assimilate all the information and ideas passed on to them by other people: teachers, playmates, pastors, other adults, including television and movie characters.

Granted, you can't keep your children within the confines of your house all their lives. But until they reach adulthood, it is your responsibility not only to find out what they are hearing and learning, but also to give them your opinion, your guidance, and your counsel on this information. There is no other way they will learn your values. Later on they will begin to decide some things for themselves, what they believe and what they don't. But as long as they live in your house, it is your responsibility to train them and encourage them to walk the paths you think are right. They may not always agree with you, but at least they will know where you stand and what you think is right. You will have fulfilled your responsibility of giving them a good foundation from which to make decisions. "Train up a child in the way he should go, and when he is old he will not depart from it" (Prov. 22:6).

The most effective way for parents to teach children is by example. You can say whatever you want to them, but your children will usually end up doing exactly what you *do*. They may love you; they may even honor you as the Bible instructs them to, but they will not respect you or believe what you say unless you live out in front of them what you say to them with your mouth. The Word of God tells us that a "child left to himself brings shame to his mother" (Prov. 29:15b). I look at the violence that consumes the youth of this world today and I grieve. I believe much of it is due to the absence of parents—their actual physical absence as well as an abdication of their spiritual headship. Children are no longer taught to respect God or even the laws of the land. They have been left to themselves. We have sown neglect and now we are reaping that harvest.

God tells us that if we do not care for our children and provide for the needs and security of our household, we have "denied the faith and [are] worse than an unbeliever" (1 Tim. 5:8). This is a parent's God-given assignment and realm of authority. But it can be lost. How does a parent lose his authority?

Losing Parental Authority

As I have stated before, authority is lost when it is abused or mishandled. Physical and emotional abuse can cause you to lose your God-given authority in the life of your child. Any adult can demand obedience from a child through physical force. Now, I do believe in proper physical discipline. But when it is excessive and is administered without love, then it is extremely counterproductive and even damaging. That obedience lasts only as long as the children remain small and defenseless. When they grow as tall as you and are no longer afraid of you, your physical force loses its effectiveness. They resent it and may even strike back at you. You can coerce children for a time, but if you don't build into those little hearts and minds the principles that go behind the correction, if you don't lead them by your own example how to live and behave properly, then you will lose your authority in their lives.

A parent can also lose his authority by undermining the God-given authority of other people in their children's lives. The parent is the final and ultimate authority in a child's life, but there are others: pastors, teachers, principals, law enforcement officers, and other adults. Every time a child hears his parent refer to a police officer as a "pig," it puts something in his little heart. It breaks down that sense of respect we all should have for authorities in law enforcement. Every time a parent speaks ill of a pastor, or says a teacher doesn't know what she's talking about, or takes a child's side unnecessarily against another adult or authority figure, it breaks down any sense of respect for authority that the child has. Eventually the child will not even respect the parent because no respect for authority of any kind has been planted in him. Remember the story of the centurion? Parents must be under authority before they can have authority. Parents must let their children see them obeying and respecting the authorities in their own lives before they can expect obedience and respect from their children.

The Authority of Civil Government

Another realm of delegated authority is civil government. Long ago rulers of countries and kingdoms were believed to be God's direct representation here on earth. These leaders ruled by what was called the "Divine Right of Kings." Monarchies were established on this principle. The people understood the concept of God granting authority to a person to rule. Today this concept has been done away with by a newer concept, one called "separation of Church and state." Originally this concept was devised to protect the Church from the state. Today that seems to have reversed a bit. Society has strayed a long way from the concept's original intention. Society today has strayed from many original concepts, and therein lies the cause of many of its problems. Nonetheless, subjects of God's Kingdom are still responsible to follow what the Bible teaches about civil government. Romans 13 gives us a clear understanding of the authority governmental leaders and law enforcement officials hold, and of how we as Christians are to respond to them.

Let every soul be subject to the governing authorities. For there is no authority except from God, and the authorities that exist are appointed by God. Therefore whoever resists the authority resists the ordinance of God, and those who resist will bring judgment on themselves. For rulers are not a terror to good works, but to evil. Do you want to be unafraid of the authority? Do what is good, and you will have praise from the same. For he is God's minister to you for good. But if you do evil, be afraid; for he does not bear the sword in vain; for he is God's minister, an avenger to execute wrath on him who practices evil (Romans 13:1-4).

Governmental leaders and law enforcement officials are the ministers of God in their particular realm of authority, according to this Scripture. So when you break civil laws or resist the authority of the government, you are not resisting people, but God, for they are God's representatives in certain areas. What are these areas, you ask?

First, they have the authority to pass and enforce laws to protect human rights. They protect you and your rights. When you choose to disobey them and the laws they pass, it is somewhat like a man who is thirsting to death but refusing water from someone. For the most part, laws are made to protect people and to preserve order. Traffic laws were not put in place simply to give police officers an opportunity to write you a ticket so they could fulfill their quota. Rather, they are in place so we won't all kill each other out on the highways and thoroughfares. Therefore, since laws exist for our ultimate good, it is to our advantage to obey them and to respect the people who pass and enforce them.

Second, governmental leaders have the authority to pass and enforce ordinances that promote the health and welfare of communities. It is their responsibility to see that the garbage is picked up and disposed of properly. It is their job to keep a fire department and a police department running in case of emergencies. It is their responsibility to ensure that the water we drink is safe and that proper regulations exist to make sure that our food is free of harmful agents. These are all the jobs of the civil government.

Third, they have the authority to collect taxes in order to maintain all these services. Some people take offense at that and even try to "cheat" on their taxes. Nevertheless, taxes are necessary. The passage in Romans continues:

> *For because of this you also pay taxes, for they are God's ministers attending continually to this very thing. Render therefore to all their due: taxes to whom taxes are due, customs to whom customs, fear to whom fear, honor to whom honor* (Romans 13:6-7).

Governmental leaders have the same authority to ask you to pay taxes as the Church does to ask you to pay tithes and give offerings. You didn't know paying your taxes was spiritual, did you? As is the pattern with the family, however, government officials also can lose their authority if they don't use it properly. So what causes the civil government to lose its authority?

Governmental Loss of Authority

Because governmental leaders are ministers of God, their actions must be consistent with the character of God. Anytime they act unjustly or unfairly toward a citizen, in a way that God would not, they lose their authority. Granted, it is part of their job to punish those who break the laws, but this punishment must be carried out fairly and must be based on a foundation that is just and equitable.

Civil government and its representatives also can lose their authority by allowing personal agendas to overshadow their sworn responsibility. When certain people are given special treatment because they are personal friends of a leader, or when others are treated less fairly for some reason that is beyond their control (e.g., racial background or economic status) and are subject to the officer or representative's personal prejudice, then that officer or representative has allowed his personal agenda to override his duty. In a more specific example, when an official or officer accepts a bribe, he allows his personal agenda, his greed for money, to keep him from doing what is right. Thus overall, civil government officials can only be considered God's ministers when they follow the ethics that their office demands in order to keep the support of the citizens. "When the righteous are in authority, the people rejoice; but when a wicked man rules, the people groan" (Prov. 29:2).

You may notice that I have not mentioned several areas over which the civil government (at least in the United States) presently has authority. That was for a reason. I believe that the civil government today is involved in some areas that it has no business being involved in. Some areas do not fall under their realm of authority, yet they have taken them as part of their authority. What areas am I talking about? These include laws dealing with abortion and prayer in schools; welfare programs; public housing policies; questions concerning people's right to die; and custody disputes over children. These are not areas for the government to be the final judge. Why, then, are they involved? The Church has abdicated her position of authority in society. All these matters should be under the jurisdiction of the Church, but the Church wouldn't handle them. So someone had to do it. Civil government stepped in. That's why we get so frustrated with our civil leaders sometimes over these questions. They are in areas that are not even supposed to be their responsibility. They're not called to do those things. These decisions are "out of their league" because they're not supposed to be in their league. We shouldn't blame them for not being able to handle these decisions properly. We shouldn't even ask them to.

The Authority of the Church

The Church is yet another area of God's delegated authority on earth. What is the role of the Church in society? The Church and its leaders are given authority to be a prophetic voice to society, to speak God's will to them. The Church's role is a priestly role, working to reconcile man to God as well as man to man. God has given the Church the authority to bring salvation, healing, and deliverance to people.

> *...and on this rock I will build My church, and the gates of Hades shall not prevail against it. And I will give you the keys of the kingdom of heaven, and whatever you bind on earth will be bound in heaven, and whatever you loose on earth will be loosed in heaven* (Matthew 16:18-19).

Matters of morality and of the heart can never be legislated by civil government because those areas are under the authority of the Church. Let me give you an example. The local church I pastor in Atlanta has an academy for boys and girls that is racially mixed, as is our congregation. The civil government tried to integrate schools years ago in the 1960's. They brought Black kids into all-White schools with armed guards. They've put Black kids on buses to go to predominantly White schools ever since. Today, in the 1990's, a student in our academy went back to public school for a year. Her first observation was that at lunchtime all the White kids sat together, all the Black kids sat together, and all the Oriental kids sat together. That's not what she had been taught at our academy. Everyone there was the same. They not only attended school in the same building and sat together in the same classes, but when social time came they were together as well. They had been taught to see each other as people and not as colors or races. Matters like these and problems in these areas will never be solved by civil government. Hearts must change along with the laws. If they don't, everyone involved is just wasting his time. Only the Church has the ability and authority to change people's hearts.

A judge should not have the authority or the responsibility of looking at a woman and telling her whether she should or should not get an abortion. That is not his place. That decision is a moral one; it is a matter of the heart that concerns an eternal soul. Only the Church has a right to speak into situations such as these. Neither can there be a blanket rule for such cases. Every situation is different with a different set of circumstances. It is ultimately the decision of the family and the Church. Civil government should not even be involved.

What is happening in our towns and cities over the issue of abortion today sickens me. Standing in the street to the point of disobeying the civil authorities at times, holding up graphic pictures and yelling in the faces of already frightened and desperate women—this is nowhere close to the character of God. Saving the lives of unborn children does not justify taking the life of another, either. What kind of sense does that make? I tell you it is nowhere close to the heart of God at all! But why has it come to this? It all started when abortion became a legal issue instead of a moral, spiritual one.

The Church needs to stand up, take its place, and speak into these situations, giving solutions. If we tell women not to have abortions, what alternative do we offer them? Years ago we began something in our local ministry here in Atlanta called "The House of New Life." Here pregnant women, especially unwed teenagers, come and live in a peaceful, healthy environment, under medical and spiritual supervision, until the birth of their baby. Then a Christian home wishing to adopt is found for this precious life. Now that's an alternative. That's a solution. Many of these girls receive their salvation there. That's the job of the Church. Government will never successfully deal with this issue.

The Church also is the only institution that is given God's authority in Heaven as well as on earth. Most areas of God's delegated authority exist within earthly boundaries, but not the Church. The civil government can punish a man for a crime he committed, but only the Church can tell him that he is forgiven of the sin of that crime. The Church has more power, and therefore more responsibility. Sadly, the responsibility often has become too great for spiritual leaders.

At one time the Roman Catholic Church was the most powerful institution in the world. It ruled over the civil government as well as over spiritual matters. But then what happened? In the Middle Ages it became corrupt. Officials had too much power and they began to abuse it. Subsequently, they lost their authority. Perhaps the Church was never meant to be responsible for the civil government. It was too great a conflict.

I am not at all saying that the Church will someday overtake civil government. That's ridiculous. There will always be a need for civil government that is separate from the Church. In the Old Testament, the prophet Samuel anointed a man to be king, the civil authority, and gave him direction and guidance. Yet once Samuel anointed him king, he left him alone unless God directed him to speak to the king on a certain matter. When God's Kingdom comes, it means only that civil government is under His authority, it follows Kingdom principles, and its laws are in accordance with the Word of God. Civil government receives guidance and counsel from the Church, but is never part of the Church or relinquishes its realm of authority to the Church.

Concerning the Roman Catholic Church, though, *Catholic* means "universal." The Catholic church is not the same as the Roman Catholic Church. The word *Roman* denoted the Roman empire; so the Catholic church added to its name and to its realm of authority a civil rule that it was never intended to govern. The basic structure of the Catholic church was correct. Yes, it became corrupt and strayed from its original, intended purpose. But it was still correct in its structure within the confines of the Church. I fear that Protestants have "thrown the baby out with the bath water" and disregarded everything about the Catholic church, even its good, of which much still remains. However, what caused the corruption in the first place? When "Roman," the dimension of civil rule, was added, they overstepped the bounds of their God-given, delegated authority. Authority is always lost when it is not used responsibly.

The Loss of Spiritual Authority

How do spiritual leaders lose their authority today? They lose their authority when they fail to represent the true character and Word of God. Spiritual leaders lose their authority by prostituting their calling—by using the Word of God deceitfully for their own personal agenda or for their private defense. They lose their authority through unrepentant conduct that causes others to lose their faith. "But whoever causes one of these little ones who believe in Me to sin, it would be better for him if a millstone were hung around his neck, and he were drowned in the depth of the sea" (Mt. 18:6). Spiritual leaders have the greatest responsibility of all to live as Jesus did. It is true that they are human and will fail, but in their hearts and in their motives they should always strive to be pure.

The Bible also deals with other realms of delegated authority. It tells us to respect those who are our teachers, how to relate to our employer, and how employers are to treat employees (e.g., see 1 Tim. 6:1-2). But the three I have dealt with in this chapter, the family, the civil government, and the Church, I believe are the most important. The Bible says, "...Every kingdom divided against itself is brought to desolation, and every city or house divided against itself will not stand" (Mt. 12:25). A city can never stand or function successfully if these three areas of delegated authority are divided and fighting each other. The successful, effective expression of the Kingdom of God on earth will occur when these three authorities support each other and work together for the common good of mankind. When these three are in harmony, then the Kingdom of God is coming to pass.

Chapter 4

The Upside-Down Kingdom

Kingdom principles seem
backwards to the natural mind.

We have seen that there must be a continuity between the various areas of delegated authority within God's Kingdom. In order to obtain this continuity, all areas must represent God in their particular realm of authority by expressing His character. As individual subjects of His Kingdom, we are called upon to do the same. How do we do this? In every situation we encounter, we ask ourselves, "What would Jesus do in this situation?" That presents another question: How do we know what He would do?

When we study Jesus' life, we begin to see patterns develop. These patterns become principles that can be applied to any situation. Many of these principles are revealed through the parables Jesus Himself used to teach His followers. As you read the parables, and as the principles emerge, you may notice that they seem unreasonable to the natural mind. You might see how Jesus' responses to things are exactly the opposite of how most of us would react in the same situation. This is why I sometimes like to refer to the Kingdom as an "upside-down" kingdom.

Jesus' Sermon on the Mount introduced us to concepts that until He preached them were never heard of—"love your enemies"; "the greatest among you shall be a servant"; "he who tries to save his life will lose it, but whoever loses his life for My sake will find it"; etc. (see Mt. 5:44; 23:11; 16:25). This is where salvation, the new birth, comes in. No man can understand the laws, concepts, and attitudes of this upside-down Kingdom with his natural mind. He has to be reborn into the Kingdom. Then with this new birth, he accepts these new laws and takes on these new characteristics.

Natural birth produces people who desire to be great. They want to be seen, heard, and respected. Sometimes they will step on whomever they have to in order to accomplish their desire. The new spiritual birth, on the other hand, produces a desire to serve others and to love the unlovable. People may tell you that you are crazy for attending church, for being baptized, for helping needy people, or for treating your enemies politely. It is crazy to their way of thinking—to the natural order of this world's system. But remember, because of Adam and Eve's rebellion, man now has a fallen nature. Self-preservation and survival of the fittest are instincts when we are born of the flesh. But when we are reborn of the Spirit, we go back to God's divine order and nature, which was lived out in the life of Jesus.

Reasonable or Unreasonable?

Some principles of the Kingdom do seem to make sense. They simply follow the law of sowing and reaping. Consider the Beatitudes: "Blessed are the merciful, for they shall obtain mercy." If you plant mercy, you reap mercy. That's not so unreasonable. But what about those principles that go against our human nature? What about those we have to work at to accomplish? We must still adhere to these principles as well, if we want to be subjects of the Kingdom.

Our whole aim in life as Christians is to be like Christ, to follow His example in all things. He told us what is required of us in order to follow him.

> *Then Jesus said to His disciples, "If anyone desires to come after Me, let him deny himself, and take up his cross, and follow Me. For whoever desires to save his life will lose it, but whoever loses his life for My sake will find it"* (Matthew 16:24-25).

Do you think taking up a cross is easy? Does denying yourself feel good? Does it make sense to the natural mind? No, of course it doesn't. It didn't seem reasonable for Jesus to have to die a criminal's death on the cross when He was the only human who had ever lived a completely sinless life. But He did it. He did something unreasonable because God asked Him to. We must follow His example.

There is an explanation even to these unreasonable and backwards principles. You simply have to look harder and dig deeper to find it. Loving your enemies and turning the other cheek (see Mt. 5:39,44) seem absolutely unreasonable. But stop and think for a moment. When you fight back with someone, you cause war. When you fight back, you create violence. But when you turn the other cheek, when you don't fight back, you disarm your enemy, and after a while you don't have an enemy any longer. You took away his power and ability to be your enemy; all the power rests with you. When a person lashes out at you, he expects to elicit a negative response from you in return. That's what he wants. If you don't give him what he wants, what he expected from you, you have rendered his attack powerless. That person doesn't know what to do next because you are not following his plan. You have the upper hand. In a way, these unreasonable, backwards, upside-down principles make ultimate sense, for they give the people who follow them the ultimate power.

Principles in Action

Let's go to the parables and see some illustrations of these principles at work. One of the most well-known parables is that of the prodigal son.

Then He said: "A certain man had two sons. And the younger of them said to his father, 'Father, give me the portion of goods that falls to me.' So he divided to them his livelihood. And not many days after, the younger son gathered all together, journeyed to a far country, and there wasted his possessions with prodigal living. But when he had spent all, there arose a severe famine in that land, and he began to be in want. Then he went and joined himself to a citizen of that country, and he sent him into his fields to feed swine. And he would gladly have filled his stomach with the pods that the swine ate, and no one gave him anything. But when he came to himself, he said, 'How many of my father's hired servants have bread enough and to spare, and I perish with hunger! I will arise and go to my father, and will say to him, "Father, I have sinned against heaven and before you, and I am no longer worthy to be called your son. Make me like one of your hired servants." ' And he arose and came to his father. But when he was still a great way off, his father saw him and had compassion, and ran and fell on his neck and kissed him. And the son said to him, 'Father, I have sinned against heaven and in your sight, and am no longer worthy to be called your son.' But the father said to his servants, 'Bring out the best robe and put it on him, and put a ring on his hand and sandals on his feet. And bring the fatted calf here and kill it, and let us eat and be merry; for this my son was dead and is alive again; he was lost and is found.' And they began to be merry" (Luke 15:11-24).

The father had every right to say, "I told you so." He had every reason to send his son away with the saying that he was the one who had left. Since the son had made his bed, he should lie in it. That is not what the father did. The father did not have the "normal" response. He didn't even make his son live like a servant, which was all the son had asked for. The old father, who every day had stood and watched for his son to come back down that road to his house, accepted his son back with loving arms and restored him to his original position.

In this parable, the father represents God. He exemplifies the nature of the King. That is the nature we too must take on; the response we must learn to give. God doesn't give up on us just because we make mistakes and get ourselves in messes. Even though He has the right to, and even though He has told us how to avoid those messes in His Word, it is His nature to forgive and to redeem. Members of the upside-down Kingdom must take on this forgiving, redemptive nature as well.

What about another story? Most of us are familiar with the incident with the adulterous woman.

Then the scribes and Pharisees brought to Him a woman caught in adultery. And when they had set her in the midst, they said to Him, "Teacher, this woman was caught in adultery, in the very act. Now Moses, in the law, commanded us that such should be stoned. But what do You say?" This they said, testing Him, that they might have something of which to accuse Him. But Jesus stooped down and wrote on the ground with His finger, as though He did not hear. So when they continued asking Him, He raised Himself up and said to them, "He who is without sin among you, let him throw a stone at her first." And again He stooped down and wrote on the ground. Then those who heard it, being convicted by their conscience, went out one by one, beginning with the oldest even to the last. And Jesus was left alone, and the woman standing in the midst. When Jesus had raised Himself up and saw no one but the woman, He said to her, "Woman, where are those accusers of yours? Has no one condemned you?" She said, "No one, Lord." And Jesus said to her, "Neither do I condemn you; go and sin no more" (John 8:3-11).

What do you think Jesus wrote on the ground? I think He began writing the sins of the accusers. Then, when they saw their sins appear, they felt convicted. How could they stone this woman when they themselves had sin in their own lives? This became a principle.

Judge not, that you be not judged. For with what judgment you judge, you will be judged; and with the measure you use, it will be measured back to you. And why do you look at the speck in your brother's eye, but do not consider the plank in your own eye? Or how can you say to your brother, "Let me remove the speck from your eye"; and look, a plank is in your own eye? Hypocrite! First remove the plank from your own eye, and then you will see clearly to remove the speck from your brother's eye (Matthew 7:1-5).

Jesus knew that those men accusing that woman had sin in their own lives. Even more than that, He knew they were the very ones who created the society in which she lived—a society in which she did what she had to in order to survive. They were just as guilty as she for the circumstance she was in. Maybe she was widowed and had children to feed, but none of them helped her or took her in. Maybe she was doing what she was to get a little money or food for her children because that was the only option left to her. Somehow Jesus knew this. So how can we apply this principle to our world today?

A young man sits in jail accused of selling drugs. Whose fault is it? His and his alone, the Pharisees would say. Maybe they would lay a little blame on his parents too. But whose fault is it really? What about the employer who wouldn't give this boy's single mother a decent job because she was a woman or because she was Black? What about the businessmen who buy the drugs—who create the market, the demand—in the first place? What about the movie producers who glamorize drug dealers on the screen for impressionable teenagers to watch? Do these people bear any of the responsibility for the circumstance of this boy? I say yes. Jesus said yes too.

Today, like the Pharisees, many say, "There's too much violence; too much crime. Lock 'em all up and throw away the key. Build more jails—bigger jails. Let 'em all go to hell. They deserve it. It's their own fault." That's not the attitude of Jesus, the One whose example we are to follow.

Life on Three Levels

There are three levels in which people operate in life. One is what I call the demonic level. At this level people give themselves over to the devil and commit unspeakable actions and crimes. When operating at this level, they have no compassion, no mercy, and no love. Another level is the human level, where people basically love those who love them, hate those who hate them, and live with the instinct for survival of the fittest. They look out for themselves and those who belong to them first, and then if it's convenient to help someone else, they will. The third level is the spiritual level. This is the level in which subjects of the upside-down Kingdom live. In this level people return good for evil; people love those who hate them and even abuse them. This is the level in which people serve others and think of others before they think of themselves.

At the spiritual level people deny themselves, take up a cross, and follow Jesus. However, as long as we are not born again into this upside-down Kingdom, as long as we live in the realm of our natural flesh, we will eventually always go back to the evil practices of our fallen nature, our human level. If things go badly enough, we might fall into that demonic level where we lose even our humanity.

When we are without salvation, we want to fight back when someone strikes us. We will want to "get even." But you see, then we must rely on our own power. If we follow Jesus and the principles He set up for us, then we can rely on His power, which is so much greater than our own. We have the ultimate power when we follow His laws because we are in control of our own emotions. Our responses don't depend on what people do to us. Thus our rewards do not depend on man and what man decides to give us on a human level. Our reward is in Heaven because we have given the power we possess back to God as He asked us to, and He will be our final rewarder.

The upside-down Kingdom demands a change of character, a change of heart. We must deny the options we have of living in the demonic or human levels of life and take on the mind of Christ. We must live in the spiritual realm.

But I say to you, love your enemies, bless those who curse you, do good to those who hate you, and pray for those who spitefully use you and persecute you, that you may be sons of your Father in heaven; for He makes His sun rise on the evil and on the good, and sends rain on the just and on the unjust. For if you love those who love you, what reward have you? Do not even the tax collectors do the same? And if you greet your brethren only, what do you do more than others? Do not even the tax collectors do so? Therefore you shall be perfect, just as your Father in heaven is perfect (Matthew 5:44-48).

How can it be possible for us to be "perfect" as God is? We are still human. How do we rise above the human level spoken of in this Scripture, where people love only those who love them and greet only those whom they consider their brothers?

God doesn't expect us to be perfect in conduct or in service, but in the motives of our heart. He wants us to be mature in loving others—even the ones who are unlovable on the human level, the ones who have mistreated us or disagree with us. We must love them as He does: unconditionally. We are to love them purely as He does, forgiving them when they make mistakes or when they sin—like the prodigal son and the adulterous woman—and restoring them as He would. That's what the upside-down Kingdom is all about—responding as God would. We do that when we follow the example He placed here on earth for us: Jesus, King of the upside-down Kingdom.

Chapter 5

Form With Power

The Holy Spirit is the transcendent power of God working through human flesh in order to change the world.

And when you pray, you shall not be like the hypocrites. For they love to pray standing in the synagogues and on the corners of the streets, that they may be seen by men. Assuredly, I say to you, they have their reward. But you, when you pray, go into your room, and when you have shut your door, pray to your Father who is in the secret place; and your Father who sees in secret will reward you openly. And when you pray, do not use vain repetitions as the heathen do. For they think that they will be heard for their many words. Therefore do not be like them. For your Father knows the things you have need of before you ask Him. In this manner, therefore, pray:

> *Our Father in heaven,*
> *Hallowed be Your name.*
> *Your kingdom come.*

Your will be done
On earth as it is in heaven.
Give us this day our daily bread.
And forgive us our debts,
As we forgive our debtors.
And do not lead us into temptation,
But deliver us from the evil one.
For Yours is the kingdom and the power
* and the glory forever. Amen.*
                                        Matthew 6:5-13

This is the prayer Jesus instructed His followers to use as the "model" prayer. It concludes with the glorious affirmation, "For Yours is the kingdom and the power and the glory forever." In the first few chapters of this book, we took a look at the Kingdom of God, how it is God's structure and the realm of operation for His authority. We saw how the Church is the expression of that Kingdom here on earth. We also saw how we, as subjects of God's Kingdom, are God's vehicle for reestablishing His order here as it once was.

The Kingdom of God, as awesome and powerful as it is, remains but a concept until it is given the power to be carried out and to come to its fruition. After Jesus' death and resurrection, He walked the earth again for 40 days. During that time He preached and taught about one thing: the Kingdom of God (see Acts 1:1-3). He wanted to make sure His followers remembered what He had taught them earlier, as well as what His whole purpose was for living and dying. After Jesus was sure they understood the structure, the Kingdom, what did He tell them?

Then He said to them, "Thus it is written, and thus it was
necessary for the Christ to suffer and to rise from the dead
the third day, and that repentance and remission of sins

should be preached in His name to all nations, beginning at Jerusalem. And you are witnesses of these things. Behold, I send the Promise of My Father upon you; but tarry in the city of Jerusalem until you are endued with power from on high" (Luke 24:46-49).

He told them to go and wait for the power, the Helper He had promised them. The Helper, the Holy Spirit, is the transcendent power of God working through human flesh (the vehicle) in order to change the world.

Empowerment for the Kingdom

When the Day of Pentecost had fully come, they were all with one accord in one place. And suddenly there came a sound from heaven, as of a rushing mighty wind, and it filled the whole house where they were sitting. Then there appeared to them divided tongues, as of fire, and one sat upon each of them. And they were all filled with the Holy Spirit and began to speak with other tongues, as the Spirit gave them utterance (Acts 2:1-4).

This was the first outpouring of the Holy Spirit in this manner, with the evidence of speaking with tongues. However, this power, this entity, was far from being new on that day. It was the very same power evidenced many times before in Israel's history, the power resident in creation from the beginning of time—the power of God Almighty. It was the power that created the heavens and the earth; that breathed life into Adam; that rolled back the Red Sea; and that resurrected Jesus from the dead. Thus the Kingdom is the structure, but the structure must be empowered.

The hand of the Lord came upon me and brought me out in the Spirit of the Lord, and set me down in the midst of the valley; and it was full of bones. Then He caused me to pass by them all around, and behold, there were very many in the open valley; and indeed they were very dry. And He said to me, "Son of man, can these bones live?" So I answered, "O Lord God, You know." Again He said to me, "Prophesy to these bones, and say to them, 'O dry bones, hear the word of the Lord! Thus says the Lord God to these bones: "Surely I will cause breath to enter into you, and you shall live. I will put sinews on you and bring flesh upon you, cover you with skin and put breath in you; and you shall live. Then you shall know that I am the Lord." ' " So I prophesied as I was commanded; and as I prophesied, there was a noise, and suddenly a rattling; and the bones came together, bone to bone. Indeed, as I looked, the sinews and the flesh came upon them, and the skin covered them over; but there was no breath in them. Also He said to me, "Prophesy to the breath, prophesy, son of man, and say to the breath, 'Thus says the Lord God: "Come from the four winds, O breath, and breathe on these slain, that they may live." ' " So I prophesied as He commanded me, and breath came into them, and they lived, and stood upon their feet, an exceedingly great army (Ezekiel 37:1-10).

God created Adam's body, and it was a beautiful and wonderful creation. It was a structure, just as the Kingdom of God is a structure. But that body lay lifeless and useless on the ground until God breathed the power of His breath into it and gave Adam spirit. Likewise, these bones lying in the valley where the prophet Ezekiel stood were dry and useless when God commanded him to prophesy to them. Then bodies came together, bone to bone, just as Christ's Body must come together as one structure: His Kingdom. Yet they must still be given that breath, that power that produces life, that allows the bodies to move and work. The Kingdom of

God must be empowered through the life-giving breath of the Holy Spirit.

The Holy Spirit Is the Power

Earlier I mentioned that the Holy Spirit is the transcendent power of God working through human flesh in order to change the world. The world is hungry for change. Proof is in the results of our 1994 national elections. The balance of power shifted from one political party to another because people want change. The people want something other than what exists now; than what they have had; than what has gotten them into the shape they are in now. What they don't know is that they are longing for the Kingdom of God. They are longing for an answer to the upheaval of our present world order, an answer which no political system can provide.

Within the last two centuries, this world has come through agricultural, industrial, educational, and technological revolutions. We could even say that we have come further in these areas in the last two centuries than in all the rest of history combined. We're smarter, healthier, better educated, better equipped, more enlightened, more civilized, and more free than man has ever been before. Yet we seem to have just as many problems, if not more, than at any other time in history. Obviously, these accomplishments and advancements are not the solution.

I marvel at the capabilities of the medical world, at the fact that we can send men to the moon, and that we can pick up a device called a telephone and speak to someone hundreds of thousands of miles away, within seconds. Computer discs can now store in one tiny chip the same amount of information that once filled thousands of pages. We are living in the age of the "information superhighway." Indeed, all these things are helpful to mankind. But what is at the heart of it all? Why have these things not brought us as far as we had hoped they might? Why can we still not live together in peace? It is because mankind as a whole still has not accepted the rule of Christ. We must learn that it is the job of the Church to show that this rule works.

The Church is to be the example of God's Kingdom on earth—to show that it will work—until everyone has had the opportunity to embrace or reject it. Then God will have some measure by which to judge the present world system. He can say to the world, "I gave you My Son to redeem you back to Myself, to My order. I gave You My Church to show you how to live under My rule by the laws of My Kingdom. If you have seen My Kingdom and have entered it, blessed are you. If you have seen and rejected it, it is now time for you to be judged."

This scenario is commonly known as the end of the age: Judgment Day. Until that time, though, the Church has a mandate to fulfill and an example to show. We do that through preaching (communicating) and demonstrating the gospel of the Kingdom by the empowerment of the Holy Spirit.

An Explosion of Power

The power of the Holy Spirit has been available to every Christian since the original outpouring on the Day of Pentecost. At the turn of this century, another great outpouring of the Holy Spirit fell, particularly on the United States, that sparked a new revival emphasizing the power of the Church. As a result, many "Pentecostal" (as they have come to be known) denominations emerged. A division arose between these churches and the more traditional, or mainline churches, which do not believe in the practice of speaking in tongues as an evidence of the indwelling of the Holy Spirit, or in the baptism of the Holy Spirit as a separate experience from salvation.

Great miracles and healings followed this movement begun at the turn of this century. It was a wonderful time in the history of the Church because God's power was again understood to be ultimate. "Church" was not just some boring, hour-long ritual that people endured to soothe their consciences or to conform to social standards. It was an opportunity to have a powerful, life-changing *experience*. People enjoyed praising the Lord, sometimes for hours on end. Thousands renewed their commitment to the Lord with impassioned conviction. In one way it was a giant step forward in the life of the Church, but unfortunately, in another way, it was also a step backward.

This explosion of power so overtook parts of the Church that they totally discarded most of their practices from the traditional Church setting. Orders of worship and any other hint of structure during a worship service were regarded as "quenching the Holy Spirit." Allowing the Holy Spirit to move in each service became the primary concern. Thus anything preplanned was considered an affront to this new move.

When I was a little boy, my daddy was one of those Pentecostal preachers. Every service began with him walking to the pulpit and asking who would like to come and sing in the choir for that service. He would wait for the choir area to fill up and then the service would begin, usually with whatever song happened to be on the mind of the pianist at the time. Suddenly there was a new virtue in spontaneity. People would often call out from the congregation to sing another verse of some song they had already finished, or people would stand up and give prophecies in tongues that would then be interpreted, usually by the pastor or an elder in the church. The singing portion of the service sometimes lasted for hours, working people up into emotional frenzies. People did things like "run the aisles," walk on the backs of the pews, or roll in the floor, hence the name "holy rollers." This type of service was often described later as "the Spirit coming down so much that the preacher couldn't even get up and preach." That part used to bewilder me. I have always thought that a service without the preached Word was a bit out of balance.

These people, my father included, were extremely sincere. They loved the Lord and had had a genuine experience with the Holy Spirit. They were good people who tried to help others. To them, this power that had consumed them was so real that they made it their exclusive aim in their services. I believe they truly felt they were following the leading of the Holy Spirit. Perhaps they were. Perhaps God had to come on just that strong during this revival of His power so people would realize again just how awesome His power is. He had to do the same thing with the Israelites. In the Old Testament we see the awesome, sometimes even fearful power of God. The Church, especially in America, had begun to be somewhat mild and static when this revival came to stir it again with God's breath, the Holy Spirit. God knew the Church would need that power to face all the changes He knew were coming in the near future.

The pendulum swings in the spiritual world just as it does in the natural world. A study of the Church from its inception, when Jesus ascended and left His followers with the Great Commission, through the years of the Roman Catholic Church, the Reformation, all the branches and phases of Protestantism, to the outpouring we have spoken about, reveals the swing of the pendulum from extreme to extreme.

What is the place of the Kingdom of God in all this? The Kingdom is the great balance. It combines what is good from every phase of the life of the Church. It takes the structure, organization, respect for authority, and the form of the liturgical, mainline churches, and blends it with the power, enthusiasm, and uninhibited praise found in the Pentecostal churches. It makes a form with power.

Chapter 6

The Prophetic Community

Truth is the standard of the
Kingdom being lived out in experience.

Because of the outpouring of the Holy Spirit that began at the start of this century, I am convinced that we are close to the culmination of the end of the age. The prophet Joel described the last events before the Day of the Lord, "Judgment Day" in this way:

> *And it shall come to pass afterward that I will pour out My Spirit on all flesh; your sons and your daughters shall prophesy, your old men shall dream dreams. Your young men shall see visions. And also on My menservants and on My maidservants I will pour out My Spirit in those days* (Joel 2:28-29).

The Church has indeed experienced and received the power of the outpouring of the Holy Spirit. Regrettably, the Church has become comfortable with the evidences of the power of the Spirit, which were once a novelty. So the questions now are: What will the Church do with this power? How will the Church use it? Will the power be selfishly kept within the Church where personally experiencing it is an end in itself? Or will it be used as a means to a greater end—to influence and change this world? The choice rests with the Church.

The Church: Salt, Light, and Seed

How will the Christian community, the Church, face the world of the next century? Will we draw together within our walls to hide from the growing violence and ungodliness? Indeed, our Christian communities should provide an environment in which our families and children can fellowship with peers in wholesome activities, where they are not under the constant barrage of non-Christian influences. These communities certainly should be made up of like-minded people, in that all members live by the covenants of Christ, the laws of the Kingdom. However, our Lord also commanded us to become "salt and light" to the world (see Mt. 5:13-14). We can, through mutual support and counsel, keep the violence and negative influences of the world at bay while still addressing the problems of society.

Remember in Chapter 3 we saw that along with authority, or power, comes responsibility. We are held responsible for sharing with the world this incredible power we have found. How do we share it? After all, the Kingdom of God is eternal. It always has been and always will be—forever. We, as humans, cannot establish it. It was established from the beginning of time and it exists in Heaven as well as on earth. Yet we *can* establish what I call "prophetic communities," which represent God's Kingdom here in the earthly realm.

The seed principle—planting seed and reaping the harvest—is a basic plan of God's Kingdom. A field can be completely desolate and unproductive, but when a farmer plants seeds in that field, sooner or later it begins to look different. Plants begin to grow. That field now possesses life. It has life because seeds contain within themselves the creative force of God. Just as the Kingdom of God is woven into the very fiber of man, it is also housed in a seed.

Seeds in a Hostile Environment

When the earth was found to be without form and void, in a chaotic condition, God's plan of recovery and restoration was to plant a seed. Into the hostile environment of the earth, God planted a seed of order and harmony and called it the Garden of Eden. When the first round of this great universal battle was lost to satan through the power of man's choice, God gave us the promise of another seed. It would be the seed of the woman that would bring final victory to mankind.

When man again began to call on God through that same power of choice, God responded by calling a pagan named Abram to pursue a life of faith. The Lord changed his name to Abraham and it was through Abraham's obedience that the promised seed was produced: Jesus Christ, the Son of God. This Seed was the very heart and personification of the Kingdom. In a day of great violence and oppression—a hostile environment—God planted a Divine Seed.

Earlier we discussed the Body of Christ, little parts of God's huge and powerful Kingdom scattered all around the world. We determined that God's Kingdom does not exist in one geographical location, but within larger, secular communities worldwide. These representations of God's Kingdom are prophetic communities, God's divine seed today.

By "prophetic communities" I certainly do not mean a "commune," or a group of people who buy a few hundred acres somewhere and draw away from "normal" society in cultish seclusion.

However, within an increasingly violent and dangerous society, prophetic communities in specific geographical locations may well become more and more popular because they will be centered around their true source of power and support: the local church.

Many of these communities will appear as lights igniting over the globe. Whatever form they take, be it a local church, a geographical neighborhood, or some other form, they will be salt and light right in the middle of the world and its affairs. You see, until the return of Christ, God's Kingdom will not rule the world. But His Spirit, through prophetic communities, will influence the world. They will act as great dragnets, bringing in all those who hear the voice of the Lord and who see demonstrated His goodness and the benefits of living in His Kingdom. Thus God has always used the principle of the seed. Whenever and wherever a hostile environment exists, there God plants a seed of His Kingdom that grows until it eventually overtakes or overcomes its hostile environment.

Biblical Precedents

Other examples of the seed principle in the Scriptures foreshadow today's prophetic communities. In the Old Testament there was the land of Goshen. There the Israelites were a community of productivity and godliness within the larger, secular community of Egypt. The Bible even says that Jewish women did not suffer greatly in childbirth during the time of their captivity as the Egyptian women did (see Ex. 1:19). The Egyptian society was carnal and ruled by an ungodly Pharaoh. However, the Jews in Goshen, though physically enslaved, were a light to the secular, Egyptian community.

Another Old Testament example of a prophetic community is Solomon's kingdom. That generation of Israelites are the ones who built the temple of the Lord in Jerusalem. They were a prophetic community because within their larger, secular community—the nations around them—they had their own community that followed spiritual authority, King Solomon, and kept the laws of the Kingdom of God. A secular queen, the Queen of Sheba, heard of this community and came to see it for herself.

> *Now when the queen of Sheba heard of the fame of Solomon concerning the name of the Lord, she came to test him with hard questions. She came to Jerusalem…and when she came to Solomon, she spoke with him about all that was in her heart. So Solomon answered all her questions; there was nothing so difficult for the king that he could not explain it to her. And when the queen of Sheba had seen all the wisdom of Solomon, the house that he had built, the food on his table, the seating of his servants, the service of his waiters and their apparel, his cupbearers, and his entryway by which he went up to the house of the Lord, there was no more spirit in her. Then she said to the king: "It was a true report which I heard in my own land about your words and your wisdom. However I did not believe the words until I came and saw it with my own eyes; and indeed the half was not told me. Your wisdom and prosperity exceed the fame of which I heard. Happy are your men and happy are these your servants, who stand continually before you and hear your wisdom! Blessed be the Lord your God, who delighted in you, setting you on the throne of Israel! Because the Lord has loved Israel forever, therefore He made you king, to do justice and righteousness"* (1 Kings 10:1-9).

It is when the Church, through prophetic communities, begins to meet the needs of people and impresses the world with its efficiency and excellence that many will be attracted to the Body of

Christ. Just as this queen did, people will begin to hear how a certain community is successfully dealing with the problems that surround them. People will begin to seek out these communities and ask them, "How do you do it?" They will be impressed, as the Queen of Sheba was, with what we have built, with the organization of our people, and most of all, with the happiness of our people. They may then want to join that particular prophetic community or go back to their own community to follow Kingdom laws and establish a prophetic community where they are. This is how the Kingdom grows and influences the world as salt and light. This is how we fulfill the Great Commission:

And He said to them, "Go into all the world and preach the gospel to every creature" (Mark 16:15).

Missions Work in Action

How do we "go into all the world" today? We do so through television, books, and radio. Yes, people can still be called to physically go to another nation to preach Jesus; that simply is not the only way we can influence the world. You see, when we do go to the nations, we must have something valuable to give them. We must do more than strive to get them "saved." Salvation is more than just going to Heaven and not to hell. Giving people salvation is showing them how prophetic communities work and how those communities finally bring about the return of Christ and the rule of God's Kingdom to earth again. True missionary work should be teaching people about what happens after salvation. Perhaps people will hear of a successful prophetic community and want someone to come to their community to teach them how to live in that manner. Whether it be in Zimbabwe or Chicago, that is "missions." I fear that too often the American Church of today is so concerned with foreign missions that people forget to preach and demonstrate the gospel to the "living creatures" in their own cities.

Part of demonstrating the gospel is demonstrating Jesus. What was the character of Jesus when He was here on earth?

The Spirit of the Lord is upon Me,
Because He has anointed Me
To preach the gospel to the poor;
He has sent Me to heal the brokenhearted,
To proclaim liberty to the captives
And recovery of sight to the blind,
To set at liberty those who are oppressed;
To proclaim the acceptable year of the Lord.

Luke 4:18-19

Jesus read these words, a prophecy from the Book of Isaiah, in the synagogue one day. As subjects of the Kingdom, we know that we must take on the character of the King, Jesus. So what will prophetic communities do? They will do exactly what Jesus did when He was here. Let me give some examples from the local church in which I minister, Chapel Hill Harvester Church. I am not intending to laud our accomplishments; we simply have had some degree of success at meeting the needs of our community, even to the point where the secular government recognized it. It all began when we started taking this Scripture seriously.

A Prophetic Community Today

About 15 years ago our church leaders became aware of the influence of drugs in our local high school. After much prayer, the concern over our young people (those in our own church and those in the community at large) inspired the start of an innovative youth ministry called Alpha. At that time a rock-and-roll Christian band was radical; something which others in our community often reminded us. But soon, every Monday night hundreds, and then thousands, of teenagers flocked to hear their kind of music—and the message of salvation and Christian living along with it.

Our church experienced phenomenal growth during this time. Not only did the young people come, but so did their parents, relatives, and even some of their teachers, all anxious to check out this place where these kids were coming and getting their lives changed.

Through the years we have tried to continue to meet the needs of the people of our community. We have a program that ministers to the chemically addicted and their families. It is called Overcomers. We began a prison ministry. We expanded our Worship and Arts department, which not only ministers to our congregation during services, but now offers Christian dance and drama events, theater for young children, and lessons of every sort at a nominal fee.

We began a job search program for those in our body who were unemployed. For those who needed job skills, we began a program as a part of our Bible Institute called "The School of Life Skills." In this program people can learn computer skills, people-helping skills, and organizational and management skills, as well as how to decorate their homes, make their own clothes, or even fish for bass.

We also addressed the problem of illiteracy in our church community as well as in our local public housing communities through our ABLE ministry. We launched special events for our elderly citizens—Super Saints, we call them. Then we founded a new program called Operation Dignity as an outreach into areas of low income public housing in Atlanta.

In our efforts to help people, did we make some mistakes? Yes, of course we did. But we continue to try to help. In fact, our city officials have often come to us during these years, asking us to teach them how we succeed at helping people in our programs. All this is an example of what the Holy Spirit can do through a people, a prophetic community of people, who sincerely want to serve

God and walk in obedience to His laws. Thus, true community begins when like-minded people, people in one accord, come together to help each other and to influence their larger community.

During the chaotic Dark Ages, when there was little or no civil government structure, communities sprang up around the great cathedrals of Europe. These areas became tiny flickering lights that tended the message of God until the world was so positioned that the gospel of the Kingdom could truly be preached to every creature.

We are now at that time, that season, when man's self-made circumstances have reached a culmination of what is possible on this earth without the leading of Jesus Christ. We have tried every kind of theory, every kind of philosophy, and every kind of government. The world groans more loudly than ever for the manifestation of the sons of God (see Rom. 8:19). The Church is the only institution where the sons of God, the sons of the Kingdom, can be manifest. So I return to the question I asked at the beginning of this chapter: What will the Church do with the power of the Holy Spirit it has received? A groaning, dying, hurting world awaits our answer.

Chapter 7

Living Water in a Dry Place

Covenant is man's opportunity
to prove God's power on earth.

Drought...famine...the stench of death. Desperately the elephants continue their search for water, their massive bodies wasting away. Already their little ones fall by the wayside. Hyenas creep in the shadows, silently choosing their next victim. All that lies before the searching elephants is an endless sea of sand and dust. Suddenly, one of the leaders stops. He starts digging at the dry land with a foot. All the others stand in confusion, but this elephant just continues to dig. He digs at that parched earth for days until, finally, he feels moisture. Still he keeps digging. Water in a desert place! Now others join him. Soon, they will literally be able to bathe in this pool.

Who told that elephant to dig? Who told him what was under that ground? If an elephant can obey an instinct like this, which God put in him, what can a people obedient to God do? God is waiting. He wants to show us where to dig. When we obey, others will run to find where the water is coming from.

I ended the previous chapter telling you about a hurting world that is waiting, whether they realize it or not, for the Church to answer the call of God to reestablish the order of His Kingdom on earth through prophetic communities. People are growing desperate for answers and solutions in their lives just as these elephants were desperate for water. The governmental systems of this world are out of answers. The people have tried the government's programs; they've worked their philosophies. Still the people search for water. They will follow whoever can help them find the water they need to survive.

Jesus came across a thirsty woman at a well one day. He told her that He could give her "living water"—water that would quench her thirst forever and become in her a fountain springing up into everlasting life (see Jn. 4:10-14). Jesus, and the salvation He offers man, is that living water that we all need. But as I pointed out before, salvation is just the beginning. Living by the laws of the Kingdom of God as a part of a prophetic community affords many benefits. These same benefits are available to every Christian and local church through the Holy Spirit, so why should I refer to them as benefits of the prophetic community? The answer is simple. I believe the concept of the prophetic community is an idea whose time has come. I believe it is the direction in which God is leading all His children because it is the best and most efficient way to both take care of the needs of local church communities and to influence the world, to reveal to them their need to embrace the laws of the Kingdom of God. Every local church that is willing, can and should become a prophetic community.

Specific Benefits in the Kingdom

When the rule of the Kingdom of God is again unchallenged on this earthly plane, there will be no sickness. There will be no more tears. Everyone will have everything he needs, and everyone will be full of joy. We are promised this in the Scriptures (see Rev.

21:4). God gives us a taste of what this will be like here and now through the prophetic community. Every time someone is healed, it serves as a reminder that perfect health is the normal course of things in the Kingdom. Every human victory we have here on earth is a foretaste of what life will be like someday if we do our job today.

Along with physical health, prayer is another benefit of the prophetic community.

> *Again I say to you that if two of you agree on earth concerning anything that they ask, it will be done for them by My Father in heaven. For where two or three are gathered together in My name, I am there in the midst of them* (Matthew 18:19-20).

No one knows why this works. It is one of those mysteries of the Kingdom. But we know that it does. So when you live in a prophetic community, you have brothers and sisters who can agree with you in prayer, as these verses say. Then what you agree on can be done, things can change, and your needs can be met! Sometimes we take for granted things that are marvelous benefits. After all, who does the atheist call on when he is sick or in need? He may have friends or family who will help him. But what happens when human resources aren't available, or when they run out? The child of God, a subject of the Kingdom, a member of the prophetic community, has the benefit of prayer always available to him.

Another benefit of the prophetic community is victory over our circumstances. God gives His sons favor and influence in the world. Doors will open for you. When other doors shut, you will know that that door led to a path God did not want you to take.

> *When you go out to battle against your enemies, and see horses and chariots and people more numerous than you, do not be afraid of them; for the Lord your God is with you,*

who brought you up from the land of Egypt (Deuteronomy 20:1).

How many times do we have obstacles and enemies that are greater than we can handle? Our enemies may not be horses and chariots, but bad emotions or estrangements. The battles we face in such areas as economics and health policies will not be solved through manmade strategies, but by the inward leading of the Holy Spirit in the lives of those who follow Him. God can change the hearts of earthly kings and rulers.

Through Him, we can do anything—but sometimes it is not in the manner in which we think it should be done. The Bible says, "He who is in you is greater than he who is in the world" (1 Jn. 4:4b). As part of this prophetic community, we see that God's ways are different than man's ways. Peace will challenge violence. Love will dispel hatred. Generosity will replace greed. Unity will displace division.

The Wisdom of the Holy Spirit

This wisdom is a benefit of the prophetic community. The Holy Spirit can teach you things and lead you in areas beyond your natural intellect or level of educational training. You can know when to speak and when to be silent. Consider the examples of Jesus and Stephen, who were both persecuted and finally put to death. When Jesus stood before Pilate, the Holy Spirit instructed Him to be quiet and not to defend Himself. But before Stephen was stoned, he knew by the Spirit that he should speak boldly to his attackers, one of whom was Saul, the man who later became the apostle Paul. In both these cases, the Holy Spirit knew which method would best serve His purposes in the lives of those who witnessed these events, especially Pilate and Saul. Whereas one would respond more to speech, the other's heart would be touched by silence. "For as many as are led by the Spirit of God, these are sons of God" (Rom. 8:14).

Now, I love education. I believe in it and have pursued it myself. But the wisdom of the Holy Spirit is far beyond anything a person can learn in a book or a classroom. I am convinced that many of mankind's great discoveries and inventions were made by people who were prompted by the Holy Spirit. Perhaps they didn't know it was the Holy Spirit at work within them, but He knew what was needed at a certain time and moved in the mind of someone to meet that need.

Today we live in a needy world. People are crying out for help, for answers, and for solutions. I believe we can meet those needs and give people the living water they crave through the wisdom and creativity of the Holy Spirit. Prophetic communities should be the most creative and productive places in the world. God is creative, and we must be creative as well.

Noah was a perfect example of what a prophetic community should be. He had never seen rain before, yet God told him the earth was to be flooded with water and instructed him to build a boat. God found someone He could trust and told him through the Holy Spirit to do something creative as a solution to a coming problem.

God has always given His people creative ideas. Remember the Hebrews down in the land of Goshen? To this day, no one has been able to figure out how the people built the pyramids. They didn't have any electrical power or any of the sophisticated equipment we have today. Yet stones weighing thousands of pounds were put on top of each other to make great tombs. The Hebrews did this with the creative ability given to them by God.

The Gift of Vision

Another benefit of the prophetic community is knowing who you are and where you are going. Your parents may not have instilled anything in you to give you confidence in yourself. Teachers, employers, and friends might have tried to convince you of your worthlessness. But if you are a child of the Kingdom, you know who you are. You are the seed of Abraham, an heir to the Kingdom of God. You are part of a loving community in which you have a specific task to accomplish.

"Where there is no vision, the people perish" (Prov. 29:18a KJV). When you fit into a purpose that is bigger than you are, you have a reason to get up every morning. If all you are living for is the hope of having a successful business, that vision will someday disappear. We hope for many temporal things, but God has created us for so much more.

Prophetic communities will be productive as well as creative. In fact, the vision of each prophetic community must be solution-oriented. It also must be made clear. Each member of the community must know exactly what the vision is all about. That way, even though individual members might suffer at times, they can still hold to the vision. Some may reap the results of wrong decisions made earlier in their lives, but with a clear vision even these people can pour out to others in the midst of their own healing. Slowly they will become a fresh stream of living water, rather than a stagnant pool of old hurts and abuses.

Joseph had every reason to become bitter and resentful. Betrayed by his brothers and thrown into a pit to die, he was sold into slavery and later imprisoned (see Gen. 37–41). What do you think kept him alive during those dark nights in that grimy old prison? He had a purpose. He may not have known anything else, but he never wavered from the vision God had given him that one day he would be a ruler. Because he listened to God and persevered, he became the "water" that saved a nation.

Sadly, most of America today does not listen to God, and so will starve in the day of famine. Yet God wants to have a people in the midst of the land who will remain prosperous and healthy during such times of famine. He wants us to face the future with confidence. To do so, though, we must remain obedient and continue to follow the leading of the Holy Spirit.

Chapter 8

With Authority
Comes Responsibility

Confidence comes from knowing you've been obedient.

We can see that God has always desired a people whom He could speak to and who would be obedient to His voice. Sometimes God could not speak because there was nobody to listen. Other times He stopped speaking because people were in disobedience. Students of the Bible know that God was silent for 400 years between the time of Malachi and the time of John the Baptist, the forerunner of Christ. Malachi cried out that the people were disobedient, that they did not heed the voice of God, and that they did not give tithes and offerings. Thus God's voice ceased. At another time in history, God stopped speaking to the priest Eli. The Lord very clearly told him why: Eli did not restrain his sons (see 1 Sam. 3:13). Eli did not have control over his household.

With authority, with power, comes responsibility. That is a point I cannot emphasize enough. Earlier in another chapter I spoke about different realms of authority that exist and how that authority could be lost if it was abused or mishandled. The prophetic community, as God's plan for the last days (in my opinion), has been given authority by God, through Jesus, to be His representative here on earth. But it involves the willing obedience of people to fulfill the responsibility that comes with the authority. Authority cannot be imposed on someone against his will. Prophetic communities will not endure unless they are led by the Holy Spirit and directed by prophetic insight. Remember, though, that human "earthen" vessels are involved in prophetic communities. Therefore there is always the possibility of error and failure. Nevertheless, we must realize that within every earthen vessel spiritually reborn into God's Kingdom lies a treasure, a gift, a calling. When every member of a prophetic community is fitly joined together and doing his specific job, then that prophetic community will be innovative, creative, and productive as a result of the Holy Spirit (power) flowing through it.

It was through disobedience in the Garden of Eden that God's order was lost in this world. It was through the total obedience of Jesus in the Garden of Gethsemane that mankind was forever forgiven and redeemed back to God. What a decisive moment it must have been when Jesus said to the Father, "Not My will, but Yours, be done" (Lk. 22:42). The Church stands at the threshold of that same decision today. God has given us His structure, the Kingdom. He has redeemed us back to Himself through the willing obedience of His Son to die on the cross. He has given us His authority and His power. Will we be strong enough, not only as individuals but also as entire communities, to say, "Not our will, but Yours, be done"? "Not our personal agenda for this local church, for this community, or for our individual lives, but Your will, God."

When any group of people in proper relationship with each other and under the headship of a godly leader says this, then that is a prophetic community. The reestablishment of God's order here on earth is one step closer to becoming reality through our willing obedience. With authority comes responsibility; we are responsible for meeting certain requirements.

Seven Requirements for a Prophetic Community

1. A prophetic community must be under command. The Bible tells us, "The steps of a good man are ordered by the Lord" (Ps. 37:23a). Being "under command" means hearing and obeying the voice of God as it is spoken through His Word and through His messengers in the Church. Unless we submit ourselves to discipline and structure, He will not direct our paths. Worldly systems will fight this directive with every force they have because they are frightened of a disciplined people. Nevertheless, these people will be disciplined to seek out and study the Word of the Lord for themselves, that they not be led into deception, and they will begin to move in one accord.

2. A prophetic community must be trustworthy. Before God will release His gifts of healing, deliverance, and miracles to a community, the people must be found to be stable. He must see if we can be trusted with financial prosperity. I've seen people arrive at our local church with everything they own in the back seat of their car. We've fed them, taught them, corrected them, and watched them prosper—only to see them become too prosperous to tithe. Too many people, when they begin to prosper through the principles they learn in God's house, want a big house. Then they must have a fancy car to go with the big house, only to discover they need a swimming pool and a membership to the country club because all the neighbors do. The kids then need tennis lessons in order to play with their friends at the country club. Pretty soon the whole family has forgotten about God, who was the One who gave them their prosperity in the first place. We see these people less and less at church on Sunday. They have the houseboat on the lake, you know, and the weekends are the only convenient time to stay there.

God does not prosper people so they can heap more things on themselves. Of course He wants His children's needs to be met and for them to be comfortable. That, however, is not the purpose of prosperity—at least not for one who is part of the prophetic community. God gives His people resources so they, in turn, can become a resource back to the Kingdom of God—back to the needy in their prophetic community who just arrived at the church with everything they own in the back seat of their car.

3. A prophetic community must be permeated by true love. God's love, agape love, is almost a missing ingredient in today's society. Most of us love only those who love us in return. God, on the other hand, is still searching for people who believe in that "upside-down" Kingdom I spoke of earlier. He is still searching for people who will love each other unconditionally. Jesus told His disciples, "By this all will know that you are My disciples, if you have love for one another" (Jn. 13:35).

Chapter 13 of First Corinthians describes the type of love Jesus was talking about:

Though I speak with the tongues of men and of angels, but have not love, I have become sounding brass or a clanging cymbal. And though I have the gift of prophecy, and understand all mysteries and all knowledge, and though I have all faith, so that I could remove mountains, but have not love, I am nothing. And though I bestow all my goods to feed the poor, and though I give my body to be burned, but have not love, it profits me nothing.

> *Love suffers long and is kind;*
> *Love does not envy;*

Love does not parade itself,
Is not puffed up;
Does not behave rudely,
Does not seek its own,
Is not provoked,
Thinks no evil;
Does not rejoice in iniquity,
But rejoices in the truth;
Bears all things,
Believes all things,
Hopes all things,
Endures all things.
Love never fails....

1 Corinthians 13:1-8

Is this the kind of love we see today among people who are supposed to be living by Christian principles? We don't even forgive each other! We hold grudges. We gossip. We speculate about people's motives.

Within what should be the unified Church Universal, we shun each other because of traditions and minor doctrinal points that divide us. We will never all agree about methods, but we must agree in spirit. If someone preaches Christ as King, then that man is my brother and I love him, unconditionally.

4. A prophetic community must implement God's direction with great boldness. In the Old Testament (2 Kings 5) there is a story of a man named Naaman. He was the commander of a great Syrian army and all the country honored him because he had just brought victory to Syria. But Naaman had leprosy, a horribly debilitating disease. However, one of his wife's servants was a young girl from—you guessed it—Israel. As an Israelite, this girl knew the power of God and believed that her master could be healed if he would only go and see the prophet Elisha. Can you imagine the courage it took for that little girl to speak to her master's wife and suggest something that must have sounded preposterous to her mistress' pagan mind? Here she was, a captive slave with no education and, because of her youth, no experience on which these people could rely. Yet something within her emboldened her to speak. Because of her boldness, Naaman was healed of leprosy.

This little girl had been raised in a prophetic community, Israel. Through a war she was displaced from her home and put into a hostile environment. Yet she was a seed of the Kingdom of God there. She brought change into her environment and was instrumental in showing those around her the power of God.

5. A prophetic community must give itself to creativity and productivity. Let's look at the example of Joseph. Can you imagine the difficulties involved in planning ahead for seven years of a famine that most people did not believe was coming? The land of Egypt was running over with plenty. Famine was unthinkable. But God had given Joseph insight into the dream of the Pharaoh, and he knew what lay ahead. Disgusted whispers must have followed Joseph everywhere he went, but he kept on doing what he knew God had told him to do. How does the story end? All the nations of the world came to Egypt when they were starving. So Joseph was prepared because he had listened to the leading of the Holy Spirit and then had been productive. He had actually done something to prepare for it. He was ready to be a resource when people were in need. This is how the prophetic community must be.

6. A prophetic community must be a giving community. Two separate mentalities concerning giving exist in the Church today. To the first group, giving something away means a reduction in their net worth. If they have a thousand dollars and give one hundred dollars away, they think of it as "only having nine hundred dollars left." They think of giving not in terms of what they may get in return, but in terms of having less than they had origi- nally. I call that the "Scarcity Mentality."

This attitude usually carries over into other areas of life as well. The people who feel this way about money feel the same way about their time. They might make statements like, "I can't sing in the choir because I can't come to rehearsal on Thursday night. I would miss my favorite television show." They never think in terms of what they will gain from doing or giving something— only in terms of what they will lose or have to give up.

On the other hand, the second group of people realize that the more they give away in time, money, and encouragement, the more they will receive back in time, money, and encouragement. This is what I call the "Abundance Mentality."

The extent to which the Holy Spirit can prosper you depends on which mentality you have. This investment principle is a diffi- cult one for Christians to understand because it does not depend on having a right spirit. It is a principle that works in all realms of life, not just in Christianity!

Look at a simple illustration. If an atheist plants a thousand acres of corn and a Christian plants one acre of corn, which one will reap the most corn? The atheist will, of course, because he planted the most. This is a law of nature that God set in motion long ago. Look at another example. Suppose an atheist and a Christian both leap off the top of the Empire State building. Will both of them reap the harvest of death? You can count on it be- cause the law of gravity is in effect.

Of course God can divinely intervene for a godly man who is praying for a good harvest. God's miracles often operate outside natural laws. If they didn't, we wouldn't call them miracles. But as a rule, if you sow scarcity, you will reap scarcity. So God is look- ing to see if there is a group of people somewhere on planet Earth who, as a community, can have an abundance mentality.

Some people don't invest time with their children, then wonder why their kids don't respect them or love them. Others spend their lives in loneliness because they haven't given themselves in friendship or shown any interest in others. God's prophetic communities will be repositories of investors. In order to get to this place where we are liberal givers of our resources and talents, we must understand and come to accept the only true motive for giving liberally: the motive of self-interest!

This doesn't sound like anything we've learned so far about the upside-down Kingdom, does it? Let's look at this issue a little more closely. God consistently uses the word *sow* in the Scriptures. *The American College Dictionary* defines this word as "to plant...for the purposes of growth" (New York: Random House, 1958). Multiplication is the principle involved here! When a gardener sows a sackful of bean seeds, he gets a truck full of beans in return. When a family sows, or invests, in blue chip stocks, that money will multiply.

God told us to put something into His Kingdom—what we sow—in order that we can get much back. It's His way of blessing us. Sometimes your harvest will be material. Always it will be spiritual. Sometimes when you give money, you get in return health, a good relationship, or peace in the midst of a troubled time. In this way you have confidence when you pray concerning these things, for you know you have sown as you were supposed to.

We like to think that we give out of love, but as human beings our love will fluctuate. We also like to think that we give out of duty, but duty falters too. Life experiences make a difference because we are, all of us, sinful people. The Bible says God knows our frame (see Ps. 103:14). He realizes that we have a survival instinct, and He uses it to help us do what He wants us to. He also is a loving heavenly Father who delights in rewarding His children when they do as He commands. I think when we understand that this self-interest is an acceptable motive for giving, though far from the only one, it takes a great burden of guilt off our shoulders. The balance to this concept is found in James 1:27. There the Bible tells us that pure and undefiled religion is to visit and care for widows and orphans who cannot give you anything in return. What you sow in them, you may reap from someone else, but you will still reap good things if that is what you sow.

7. A prophetic community must be a community of purpose. True community, which reflects God's character and walks by His Spirit, has the purpose of ushering in the Kingdom of God. Although we do not establish the Kingdom (it is eternal), we do have a role to play in pointing others to it. Whatever God gives us to do to be salt and light to a hurting world, we must do. We each must have a personal vision for the purpose of our individual lives within our prophetic community, as well as know the corporate vision of our community.

What is your vision within your prophetic community? Do you know? Knowing the purpose for your life as an individual is very important. Even if you live in a successful, functioning prophetic community, that community is still within the larger, secular community of this world. Sometimes that world can be harsh; sometimes it holds heartache and sorrow for us. Knowing your purpose can keep you going at times when nothing else will. Joseph's personal vision and purpose kept him going when he was sold into slavery, and when he was falsely accused and imprisoned. John the Baptist's vision kept him preaching, even when he was in the wilderness and no one seemed to be receiving his message. Our hopes, dreams, and personal ambitions can fail us at times and leave us feeling empty when they don't come to pass. But if God has given you a purpose for living, know that His Word will not return void.

> *For as the rain comes down, and the snow from heaven, and do not return there, but water the earth, and make it bring forth and bud, that it may give seed to the sower and bread to the eater, so shall My word be that goes forth from My mouth; it shall not return to Me void, but it shall accomplish what I please, and it shall prosper in the thing for which I sent it* (Isaiah 55:10-11).

What if God taps you on the shoulder and chooses you to suffer for His Kingdom? How will you respond? Many of us want to be chosen if it means sitting on a throne giving orders or if it brings us great notoriety. Being chosen of God, being part of the prophetic community, however, sometimes entails suffering.

I asked earlier if the Church as a community was ready to pray the prayer Jesus prayed in the Garden, "Not My will, but Yours." We must all personally ask ourselves that same question. Are we willing to do whatever it takes to be a part of the prophetic community, to be part of that mature Bride Jesus will return for?

Suffering for God

How may you be called upon to suffer? Maybe you'll be persecuted. Your family may jeer at you and call you a fool for spending all your time in church. Perhaps your accountant will question why you give so much of your money to the cause of God. Perhaps your co-workers will laugh at you for not taking part in their "happy hour" after work. Will you be intimidated? Or will you be a seed of the Kingdom in a hostile environment, a light permeating the darkness in the world around you?

When I was a young college graduate, preaching on the weekends and working in a factory during the week to pay for seminary,

I cannot tell you how much I was laughed at. I was the only worker in my whole crew who openly admitted to being a Christian. I worked in a dye factory and we had to work around huge, hot vats all day long. When I would leave the others to go to the restroom, I could hear the others laughing about my "sanctimonious ways" because I wouldn't laugh at their dirty jokes or enter into filthy, degrading talk about women.

Then one day one of them said to me, "Earl, I just found out that my mother is dying of cancer. Will you say a prayer for her?" I ended up leading all but one of those crew members to Jesus. Two of them later became preachers. But it was all because I allowed myself to suffer their laughter and insults and not let it change my attitude or character. I had to persevere just as the prophetic community must persevere—just as some of you must persevere daily in your workplaces. Faithfulness in the time of persecution is a form of suffering. This is what is meant by "turning the other cheek."

Neither does witnessing and standing up boldly for what you believe in mean being rude or obnoxious. The Holy Spirit is a gentleman; He woos people. You don't draw people to Jesus by being offensive. Recently I was called upon to give the invocation at a luncheon for the Governor of Georgia. He knew that I had opposed the lottery in Georgia, which was one of his projects, and he seemed to be a bit leery of what I was going to say.

When I got up to make a few remarks before the prayer, I said something like this: "It's a real honor to be here, and although the governor and I have disagreed on a topic or two, I just want to say that if he has the winning lottery ticket, I'll be happy to accept it for the church."

That made him and everyone else laugh, and it broke the ice and tension. After the luncheon I talked with the governor and told him I'd like to have some input about how the lottery is marketed on television and how the money is appropriated. Do you know what happened? I got an appointment with him to discuss those very things.

Do you think I would have gotten that opportunity of influence if I had stood up and made some stiff, pious remarks about something that was then out of my power to change? Certainly not. I still don't like the lottery, but because I was gracious rather than offensive, there is now an open door to temper a situation as well as an opportunity to nurture a relationship with the governor.

That's the way we influence the world. The strategy of God's Kingdom is love. We do not go out to conquer and take over; we go out to serve and accommodate others as much as lies within our power. The Scriptures direct us to be "wise as serpents and harmless as doves" (Mt. 10:16). Our objective is to influence people in a positive way and show them the attractiveness of the prophetic community. When we are perceived as judgmental and uncompromising, we lose our advantage.

We are also told in Scripture that, in this world, we may have to give up some things. If you lose something in the process of suffering for the Kingdom of God, I urge you not to look at the loss, but at the promise.

And everyone who has left houses or brothers or sisters or father or mother or wife or children or lands, for My name's sake, shall receive a hundredfold, and inherit eternal life (Matthew 19:29).

Philippians 3:10 says, "That I may know Him and the power of His resurrection, and the fellowship of His sufferings, being conformed to His death." We tend to play games with God until we reach this level of sacrifice and obedience. To truly make the prophetic community work, though, we must be dead to ourselves and alive to God and His purposes. Everyone who was called on to suffer in the Bible was given a choice to do it or not. Esther had a choice; Jonah had a choice; Moses had a choice—even Jesus had a choice. So we must come to the place where we realize that the choices we make are our witness to the world. Those who are chosen to suffer will always have the opportunity to say no. God doesn't force this level of service on anyone. But if we suffer through willing obedience, we will reap great rewards in the end.

We also must realize that if we suffer with Christ, we will also reign with Him (see 2 Tim. 2:12 KJV). Sometimes suffering is necessary to bring about God's purposes in the world. Therefore we as members of the prophetic community must keep our focus on the eternal perspective, knowing that this life is but a moment as compared with the rest of time. When we know that, it helps make us willing, no matter what it takes, to suffer.

The Spirit Himself bears witness with our spirit that we are children of God, and if children, then heirs—heirs of God and joint heirs with Christ, if indeed we suffer with Him, that we may also be glorified together. For I consider that the sufferings of this present time are not worthy to be compared with the glory which shall be revealed in us (Romans 8:16-18).

Chapter 9

The March

**The mission is to march toward
the glorious destination of the Kingdom of God.**

"We're marching to Zion
Beautiful, beautiful Zion
We're marching upward to Zion
The beautiful city of God."

"We're Marching to Zion"
written by Isaac Walts and Robert Lowry

So often I have heard that song; it's been popular in Pentecostal circles since the days of my childhood. That song, along with many others like it, contains a powerful message that I'm afraid many in the Church have misunderstood. This "march" or journey has too often been characterized by the Church as a taxing, toilsome trek through an alien and hostile land.

Granted, trying to abide by Christian principles in the climate of today's society can prove to be difficult. As we've already discussed, the environment can indeed be hostile at times. However, the biggest problem lies in what we choose to emphasize. Many happy and successful people became so by concentrating on what they wanted—the positive—instead of what they lacked—the negative.

Looking at ourselves as weary pilgrims barely able to put one foot in front of the other; asking God only for enough strength to make it day by day, so we can dodge all the fiery darts of the enemy; looking to the day when we will arrive at the gates of Heaven where we can lay down all our incredibly heavy burdens and finally receive that jeweled crown from Jesus—this is not what I would call victorious Christian living. It's no wonder we have not attracted more people to the Church, not when this attitude is still prevalent in a good portion of it. Most people's answer to this attitude is, "I don't know what world you're living in, but the one I'm living in is a lot of fun!"

The whole point of Chapter 7 showed that the prophetic community must become the living water to the world. We must become attractive to people not only when they are in trouble, but also when everything is fine. The Church has always concentrated on helping those who are hurting and helpless, and rightfully so. We must never lose our compassion for those in need. At the same time, however, we must remember that we are called to be salt and light to the *whole* world.

Yes, there are many needy people, but there are also many who are successful. Sometimes the successful ones are harder to reach simply because they don't feel they "need" anything more than what they already have. We must do the best we possibly can to show them the abundance, creativity, productivity, health, and happiness of the prophetic community. Success and excellence always draw people. They are the keys we must use to show people that the glory of the presence of the Lord is much more fulfilling than anything they can ever experience or possess in the natural realm. However, we must first know it for ourselves. Then we can allow our vision to inspire others to enlist in our march toward the glory that is in that eternal city, Zion, the Kingdom of God.

Our Eternal Destination

The Book of Revelation gives us a panoramic view of God's vision for humanity. Nowhere else in the Bible is there a greater picture of the glory to come when Christ returns to rule and reign. The apostle John attempted to describe the indescribable in human terms:

> *And he carried me away in the Spirit to a great and high mountain, and showed me the great city, the holy Jerusalem, descending out of heaven from God, having the glory of God. Her light was like a most precious stone...* (Revelation 21:10-11).

This is our destination. Our march will at times be grueling; we will suffer pain and hardship. But instead of focusing on the suffering, let us keep our eyes on the glory that is set before us. Let us realize that even while we are on this journey, we can live victoriously as overcomers in this life, as crusading conquerors on a mission, rather than despondent slaves carrying out a sentence.

The thread of God's mission for us runs throughout the Bible. All along God has been trying to point us toward His order and design within a world filled with contention and strife. On the other hand, satan's great mission is to distract us from the purpose God wants us to accomplish. What do we do? In the natural world, when we want to make sure we reach our destination without being "distracted" down wrong roads, we use a map. For our spiritual journey, the Bible is the map that shows us the route to Zion, and contains many signs for us to follow.

Our Spiritual Road Signs

The first sign to mankind along the journey to Zion is seen in the lesson learned from the Garden of Eden: God was trying to point us, through obedience, toward reclaiming order and design out of disorder and rebellion.

The next sign we see is mankind crying out to God! When Adam's sons realized what they had lost, "then men began to call on the name of the Lord" (Gen. 4:26b). Sometimes God backs away when people want to do things their own way in disobedience to Him. Sooner or later, though, they realize their need for a higher power and call out. Today God is always there for man, even as He was then. Thus Abraham is the next major signpost, for he became the father of the household of the faithful through his ability to believe God. He was the first step back toward obedience after the fall of man through disobedience in the Garden. Following him, Israel became God's chosen people. So the obedience of one man (Abraham) progressed to the obedience of an entire nation. Centuries later, John the Baptist proclaimed the coming of the Christ. Jesus Christ is the heart of Zion. He is *the* signpost.

Jesus said to him, "I am the way, the truth, and the life. No one comes to the Father except through Me" (John 14:6).

Pentecost, with the outpouring of the power of God, is another major signpost. Our incarnate God left us, but He promised that when He departed, His Holy Spirit would come and would never leave us. Thus the journey progresses, and with each new landmark we pass, we come closer and closer to the eternal city.

The last signpost that Jesus left is the Church.

...on this rock I will build My church, and the gates of Hades shall not prevail against it (Matthew 16:18).

That is where we, with a renewed vision of God's eternal mission, come in. In the light of these major signs, it is amazing that there are still those who resist the concept of dynamic prophetic communities redeeming the hurting masses of humanity. It is as if people have a reluctance to "presume" to do God's work. Of course God could accomplish His objective here on earth without us, but we are clearly a part of His plan because He loves and wants us, not because He needs us! It is our need for Him, and our demonstration that He is the only solution to every care and woe, that He is concerned about.

The Preparing Bride

In the Scriptures, just before John describes "the great city" that has "the glory of God," an angel says, "Come, I will show you the bride, the Lamb's wife" (see Rev. 21:9-11). The Church Universal is this Bride. The Bridegroom is Jesus. His Second Coming is their union, or wedding. It is at that great wedding feast, after the Church in the role as the Bride says, "Come!" that we will enter into the Glory of the Lord (see Rev. 22:17). The Glory of the Lord will be when Jesus puts an end to all rule, authority, and power of the enemy; when death is conquered! Then, just as a woman is a helpmeet to her husband, so the Church, Christ's Bride, will be present by His side, having done her part in helping Him when He delivers the Kingdom of this world back to God the Father.

Think about this relationship between Christ and the Church as Bride and Bridegroom. When two people are to be married, who accepts the proposal when the bridegroom declares his love? The bride does! Likewise, Jesus has declared His love for us and has asked for our hand. He has asked us to be His helpmeet to complete the mission He was sent to accomplish. It is now up to us, the Church, His Bride, to answer and to prepare ourselves for this eternal life together with Him in glory.

Our marching orders while we are traveling this journey and making our final preparations are simple, but they are not easy. We must first lift up Jesus Christ, who is the King of kings and Lord of lords, and avoid anything that does not have His character. We must worship the Lord in spirit and in truth. We must be obedient to His laws, to His covenants, and to His vision. We must learn to give freely, not always expecting reciprocation. We must pray and fast before God alone, not to be seen and heard by man. Finally, we must learn to lay up treasures in Heaven and not hoard them here on earth. (See John 4:24; Matthew 10:8; 6:16-19.)

We've discussed at length this period of preparation as it becomes manifest to us through the vision for each prophetic community. Now that the wedding date draws near, the activities grow more intense. Things always get hectic right before a wedding— personalities clash; tempers flare. Similarly, in the Church during these last days, more and more we see division, strife, betrayal, and immaturity.

Nonetheless there will always be a light, even if only a glimmer, of God's glory on this march to Zion. The Kingdom of God is our native land, just as the fullness of his father's homeland was native to the prodigal son. Sadly, the glitz and glitter of satan's counterfeit society has lured many away from their true purpose. Those who have followed satan's path may now be living in the lap of luxury, or in the hogpens of this world, just as that prodigal son did. But our Father God has a calling and a purpose for each and every life. It is our job to seek them all out and point them toward their true homeland, the glorious Kingdom of God.

Chapter 10

The Homeland

**The Kingdom of God is not offered
to the good or the worthy—but to the willing.**

A young man lies face down at the edge of a muddy pool. He hasn't eaten anything but scraps for days. Wearing the same clothes he arrived in one month ago, he smells of the rot and filth that surround him. His bones ache from sleeping on the ground. Now sleeping restlessly, he dreams of his father, whose house is warm and comfortable, and abundant with food. He sees the smiling faces of his brother and mother sitting together in the evening, telling stories to each other. With a jolt he awakens to the sad reality of stench and hunger. Tears slowly trickle down his face. The gnawing in the pit of his stomach is more than natural hunger. He is homesick.

Crying openly now, sorrow and regret rush over him in great waves. His body heaves with emotion one last time—then the sobbing stops. He has made a decision. No matter what it takes, he is going home. He will apologize to his father and beg to be just a servant in his house. For even the servants in his father's house have enough to eat and enjoy a roof over their heads.

So begins the parable of the prodigal son, a familiar story found in Luke 15 that I have mentioned before. We know that the son was a young man who couldn't wait to be out on his own, so he asked his father to give him his inheritance early. Then he took the money and left his father's house, going out to make his own way in the world. He was young and foolish, and away from the safety and wisdom of his father, the money soon ran out. When that happened, his newly made "friends" left him. Thus the son was left without food, shelter, or friends. He had to depend on the mercy of a stranger who allowed him to live with his pigs and eat what they ate in exchange for feeding and caring for them. The once prosperous heir of a mighty household was reduced to feeding hogs and living like them. What happened?

This prodigal son is symbolic of many today who think they don't need God in their lives. They feel that the Church is an irrelevant dinosaur that has nothing to offer them or their families. Sometimes people can make it without God...for a while. But we know there is no salvation at the end of their lives. Long before their end comes, most wind up like this son, living in either a physical or emotional "hogpen" where they do not reach their potential, feel miserable, and sense a great void exists in their lives— a hunger for something they can't define. These people are convinced that they can make their own decisions in life and don't need the spiritual authority that rests in the Church. Still the void grows larger and they begin their search for something to fill it. As temporary solutions fade away, many realize the only true and lasting solution is Jesus.

The Birthright

In the days of the Old Testament, the oldest male in every household possessed what was called the birthright. He had full right to all his father's inheritance. Genesis 25 recounts a story of Esau and his younger brother, Jacob, that involves this birthright:

Now Jacob cooked a stew; and Esau came in from the field, and he was weary. And Esau said to Jacob, "Please feed me with that same red stew, for I am weary."... But Jacob said, "Sell me your birthright as of this day." And Esau said, "Look, I am about to die; so what is this birthright to me?" Then Jacob said, "Swear to me as of this day." So he swore to him, and sold his birthright to Jacob. And Jacob gave Esau bread and stew of lentils; then he ate and drank, arose, and went his way. Thus Esau despised his birthright (Genesis 25:29-34).

Esau sold his birthright. He gave up the inheritance that was rightfully his. Just like the prodigal son and so many of us today, Esau got himself in a position where he was so desperately hungry and empty that he would do anything for some relief from his pain. This is exactly the position satan wants us in: settling for scraps when all the riches of our Father's house await us in His Kingdom. It is a position from which we can't see the folly of giving away all we have been rightfully promised as heirs of God's Kingdom—for one little bowl of soup when we're hungry; for one more high; for one more drunken stupor so the pain can go away a little while longer.

God's Kingdom—the entrance into the eternal city of glory, Zion—is promised to every creature if he will but accept by faith the gift of redemption Jesus offered through His death on the cross. The Kingdom is our homeland. It is what each of us longs for deep inside, to again be one with our Creator, living in the safety and peace that He provides.

Eternal Life in Glory—The Kingdom of God

The wonderful thing about eternal life in Glory is that it is not reserved just for the good or the worthy. It is offered to the willing.

That is the principle behind the cathedral that the local church which I minister at built to worship in. The very first message I ever preached in that pulpit was entitled "Whosoever Will." This cathedral is open to anyone and everyone. We are not allowed to pick and choose who can be ministered to within these walls. This building doesn't belong to us. God told us to build it and we are now merely its caretakers. I think many of us will be surprised at who makes it to Heaven. We are finite beings struggling to understand the ways of an infinite, eternal God.

For the kingdom of heaven is like a landowner who went out early in the morning to hire laborers for his vineyard. Now when he had agreed with the laborers for a denarius a day, he sent them into his vineyard. And he went out about the third hour and saw others standing idle in the marketplace, and said to them, "You also go into the vineyard, and whatever is right I will give you." So they went. Again he went out about the sixth and the ninth hour, and did likewise. And about the eleventh hour he went out and found others standing idle, and said to them, "Why have you been standing here idle all day?" They said to him, "Because no one hired us." He said to them, "You also go into the vineyard, and whatever is right you will receive." So when evening had come, the owner of the vineyard said to his steward, "Call the laborers and give them their wages, beginning with the last to the first." And when those came who were hired about the eleventh hour, they each received a denarius. But when the first came, they supposed that they would receive more; and they likewise received each a denarius. And when they had received it, they complained against the landowner, saying, "These last men have worked only one hour, and you made them equal to us who have borne the burden and the heat of the day." But he answered one of them and said, "Friend, I am doing you no wrong. Did you not agree with me for a denarius? Take what is yours and go your way. I wish to give to this last man the same as to you. Is it not lawful for me to do what I wish with my own things?..." So the last will be first, and the first last. For many are called, but few chosen (Matthew 20:1-16).

God is the Creator of everything that exists. It is His right to do what He wants with His own things, just like the landowner in the parable. God's time is not our time and His ways are not our ways. We who have been Christians for a long time must not let ourselves fall into the trap these workers did of becoming jealous and disgruntled at the very people whom we should help.

Jesus said to them, "My food is to do the will of Him who sent Me, and to finish His work. Do you not say, 'There are still four months and then comes the harvest'? Behold, I say to you, lift up your eyes and look at the fields, for they are already white for harvest! And he who reaps receives wages, and gathers fruit for eternal life, that both he who sows and he who reaps may rejoice together. For in this the saying is true: 'One sows and another reaps.' I sent you to reap that for which you have not labored; others have labored, and you have entered into their labors" (John 4:34-38).

Remember the worldwide Body of Christ set up through prophetic communities? They are exactly what this passage of Scripture is referring to. Every person, from the inception of the early Church until now, who has yielded in obedience to the will of God as Jesus did, has had a part in the great harvest that will come before the end of the age. Those who complete the work will have done their share, just as those who began it. We will all reap the same reward, eternal life in Glory, our native homeland—the Kingdom of God.

Now the wall of the city had twelve foundations, and on them were the names of the twelve apostles of the Lamb. And he who talked with me had a gold reed to measure the city, its gates, and its wall. ... Then he measured its wall: one hundred and forty-four cubits, according to the measure of a man, that is, of an angel. The construction of its wall was of jasper; and the city was pure gold, like clear glass. The foundations of the wall of the city were adorned with all kinds of precious stones.... But I saw no temple in it, for the Lord God Almighty and the Lamb are its temple. The city had no need of the sun or of the moon to shine in it, for the glory of God illuminated it. The Lamb is its light. And the nations of those who are saved shall walk in its light, and the kings of the earth bring their glory and honor into it. Its gates shall not be shut at all by day (there shall be no night there). And they shall bring the glory and the honor of the nations into it (Revelation 21:14-15,17-19, 22-26).

For Thine is the Kingdom, the power, and the glory, forever!

Chapter 11

Forever and Ever

**The willing obedience of a remnant
is the means for the success of God's plan.**

Eternity is a concept difficult for us to comprehend with our finite human minds, yet we all contemplate its meaning at some time during our lives. We read a passage in the Bible such as, "In the beginning God..." and we automatically think things like: When was the beginning? Who created God? What existed before God, if anything? At the opposite end of the spectrum, it is just as difficult to think of our spirit living on eternally—as long as time shall last, without end. How long is forever? We can't begin to know these things, and have no means of obtaining the information, apart from God Himself. Because our minds are limited to the confines of a concept such as "time," we must deal with time as we know it.

The Plan From the Beginning

What do we think of as "the beginning of time"? Most Christians consider God's creation of Adam and Eve to be the beginning

---

of human time because it marks the beginning of His interaction with humanity. As we discussed earlier, God had a plan when He created Adam and Eve. There had been rebellion in the universe and He planned for this new creation of His to overcome the rebellion lucifer had begun and put an end to it. But as we have also seen, the plan in the Garden of Eden was disrupted when man sinned. What was left for God to work with? Freedom of choice. The free will He had placed within His creation still existed. So depending on this human freedom of choice, He set the plan in motion again.

Sadly, once again sin and violence covered the earth—so much so that God could find only one righteous man, Noah.

> *Then the Lord saw that the wickedness of man was great in the earth, and that every intent of the thoughts of his heart was only evil continually. And the Lord was sorry that He had made man on the earth, and He was grieved in His heart. So the Lord said, "I will destroy man whom I have created from the face of the earth, both man and beast, creeping thing and birds of the air, for I am sorry that I have made them." But Noah found grace in the eyes of the Lord* (Genesis 6:5-8).

From the time after the fall of Adam and Eve to Noah's time, God depended on man to do His will and follow His laws willingly, based on man's freedom of choice. Still wickedness eventually prevailed. Finally there was only one man, Noah, who followed the Lord willingly. Thus God destroyed with a great flood everything except this one righteous man and his family. Mankind again had a chance to begin with a clean slate. Just as Adam and Eve had the mandate to multiply and fill the earth, Noah's family now had the opportunity to replenish the earth with righteous people. Yet once again sin and unrighteousness prevailed and man's second opportunity to fully overcome rebellion in the earth was lost.

> *These were the families of the sons of Noah, according to their generations, in their nations; and from these the nations were divided on the earth after the flood. Now the whole earth had one language and one speech. And it came to pass, as they journeyed from the east, that they found a plain in the land of Shinar, and they dwelt there. Then they said to one another, "Come, let us make bricks and bake them thoroughly." They had brick for stone, and they had asphalt for mortar. And they said, "Come, let us build ourselves a city, and a tower whose top is in the heavens; let us make a name for ourselves, lest we be scattered abroad over the face of the whole earth." But the Lord came down to see the city and the tower which the sons of men had built. And the Lord said, "Indeed the people are one and they all have one language, and this is what they begin to do; now nothing that they propose to do will be withheld from them. Come, let Us go down and there confuse their language, that they may not understand one another's speech." So the Lord scattered them abroad from there over the face of all the earth, and they ceased building the city. Therefore its name is called Babel, because there the Lord confused the language of all the earth; and from there the Lord scattered them abroad over the face of all the earth* (Genesis 10:32–11:9).

Upon the first reading, this story may be confusing. The people were in unity and through that unity of purpose they accomplished something great. So why did God destroy it and scatter them? He did so because of their motivation for doing it. Rebellion had again crept into mankind. The key appears in Genesis 11:4: "let us make a name for ourselves." They were not building this tower and city to glorify God. They were building it to glorify themselves. This is the very attitude lucifer had when he proclaimed, "I will exalt my throne above the stars of God...I will be like the Most High" (Is. 14:13-14). Men had become gods unto themselves. They used the tools God had given them—their natural abilities, wisdom, and common language—to accomplish something great, and then had not thanked Him for His help or even acknowledged that it was those God-given gifts that allowed them to achieve such a feat. Again, another opportunity is dashed and God provides another.

Until this time God had depended on man's free will—yet time after time man disappointed Him. God next planned to overcome rebellion by restricting man through Moses' Law. Specific guidelines were given to man because he had proven that he could not live a righteous life without clearly set boundaries that were strictly enforced. In Exodus 20:1-17 the Ten Commandments were given to the people through Moses. But even within these restraints mankind did not overcome rebellion and sin. Many prophets who came after the law warned, pleaded, and beseeched the people—but to no avail.

The Law and the Seed

Finally, the only things God had left were Himself and His seed principle. He had planted a seed within Abraham long before the law was given that Abraham would be the father of a faithful nation. The promise of that seed was still alive, and it became God's final weapon against rebellion.

Now to Abraham and his Seed were the promises made. He does not say, "And to seeds," as of many, but as of one, "And to your Seed," who is Christ. And this I say, that the law, which was four hundred and thirty years later, cannot annul the covenant that was confirmed before by God in Christ, that it should make the promise of no effect. For if the inheritance is of the law, it is no longer of promise; but God gave it to Abraham by promise. What purpose then does the law serve? It was added because of transgressions, till the Seed should come to whom the promise was made; and it was appointed through angels by the hand of a mediator. Now a mediator does not mediate for one only, but God is one. Is the law then against the promises of God? Certainly not! For if there had been a law given which could have given life, truly righteousness would have been by the law (Galatians 3:16-21).

God gave Abraham a promise. Out of that promise the nation of Israel was birthed. Even though they, as a nation, were faithful to God to some extent, sin and rebellion still existed. The obedience they did have was not enough to be that final witness to the world so judgment could come. As we just read in the Scripture from Galatians, the law was not given to annul God's promise to Abraham. It was given because the people fell into transgression again. The law was only a means of keeping the people obedient until the true Seed of Abraham, Jesus Christ, arrived. It was merely a step in God's final plan. Jesus Christ, the very Son of God Himself, is God's final method of bringing man out of rebellion and redeeming him unto Himself. Several Scriptures bear out this truth:

But before faith came, we were kept under guard by the law, kept for the faith which would afterward be revealed. Therefore the law was our tutor to bring us to Christ, that we might be justified by faith. But after faith has come, we are no longer under a tutor (Galatians 3:23-25).

Do not think that I came to destroy the Law or the Prophets. I did not come to destroy but to fulfill. For assuredly, I say to you, till heaven and earth pass away, one jot or one tittle will by no means pass from the law till all is fulfilled (Matthew 5:17-18).

If the law could have made people live righteously and given them life, there would have been no need for anything beyond the law. But even the law didn't accomplish what God wanted. There was still the question of man's free will. With the law as the boundary, free will was somewhat, although not totally, taken away. "For the letter kills, but the Spirit gives life" (2 Cor. 3:6b). God still longed for "willing obedience"—for followers who did not act like robots programmed and conditioned through the law.

There is therefore now no condemnation to those who are in Christ Jesus, who do not walk according to the flesh, but according to the Spirit. For the law of the Spirit of life in Christ Jesus has made me free from the law of sin and death. For what the law could not do in that it was weak through the flesh, God did by sending His own Son in the likeness of sinful flesh, on account of sin: He condemned sin in the flesh, that the righteous requirement of the law might be fulfilled in us who do not walk according to the flesh but according to the Spirit (Romans 8:1-4).

Through Jesus, God joined Himself to mankind. He poured all of Himself into Jesus. Thus through Jesus God became more than a creative spectator in man's world; He became a participant in His own universe. At that point it was possible for God Himself to feel human emotions, to be tempted as we are. With the birth of Jesus, God became inseparably connected to man. The verdict is still out whether this final attempt will succeed or fail. If it succeeds, the result will be the realization of the Kingdom of God. If it fails because all human beings reject the new life available in Jesus Christ, we risk losing the earth again to satan's control, when sin and rebellion again will reign.

It Is Up to Us

Adam and Eve were God's first human creation. Then mankind got a fresh start with Noah and his family. We also were given the opportunity to overcome rebellion when we were given the law. But the final opportunity lies before us in the person of Jesus Christ. We all have the opportunity to become new creatures through His salvation.

Therefore, if anyone is in Christ, he is a new creation; old things have passed away; behold, all things have become new (2 Corinthians 5:17).

The final plan, that of God joining Himself to humanity through Jesus Christ, is now in place to purge and restore the earth. If you are a part of this plan, you are a new creation and become a minister of reconciliation.

We then, as workers together with Him also plead with you not to receive the grace of God in vain. For He says: "In an acceptable time I have heard you, and in the day of salvation I have helped you." Behold, now is the accepted time; behold, now is the day of salvation (2 Corinthians 6:1-2).

Every person who calls himself a Christian is now a worker together with God in His final plan to overcome rebellion and to redeem this earth unto Himself. It is our job—the job of the Church—to proclaim that now is the acceptable time for the salvation of the world. Will the plan work? What about freedom of choice? Will it ever be possible for even a remnant of mankind to become willingly obedient to God's will without the restraint of the law? Those are the questions the Church faces today.

What are the obstacles to this plan? Obviously, the main obstacle is us—humans—because of our fallen human nature. Because of the constant presence of rebellion and sin in the world, we have allowed the original plan of God to be prostituted time after time—even after God has given us chance after chance to overcome sin and rebellion. As I stated in the Introduction, this world has become a place of violence, greed, lust, selfishness, warfare, and hatred. It has become such a place because those things are the results of sin and rebellion. "For the wages of sin is death..." (Rom. 6:23). If this final plan of God fails because the Church fails to be willingly obedient to God's will, it means the eventual death of mankind. As depressing a spectacle as this is, we are not without hope. The rest of Romans 6:23 reads: "...but the gift of God is eternal life in Christ Jesus our Lord."

We, the Church, will determine the fate of humanity. In an earlier chapter I asked the question about a remnant of people becoming totally and willingly obedient to God's will without the restraint of the law. I was speaking of prophetic communities. I believe they are this remnant that can, in these last days, aid the success of God's final plan. Perhaps it is impossible for every single human on the face of the earth to become "willingly obedient." Perhaps it is impossible for the institutional Church as well. But perhaps God is only looking for a remnant, as He did in the cities of Sodom and Gomorrah.

> *And Abraham came near and said, "Would You also destroy the righteous with the wicked? Suppose there were fifty righteous within the city; would You also destroy the place and not spare it for the fifty righteous that were in it? Far be it from You to do such a thing as this, to slay the righteous with the wicked...." So the Lord said, "If I find in Sodom fifty righteous within the city, then I will spare all the place for their sakes"* (Genesis 18:23-26).

Just as Abraham pleaded for the righteous in the cities of Sodom and Gomorrah, so Jesus intercedes for the righteous in this world. Prophetic communities throughout the earth represent the righteous. As members of these prophetic communities, it is our job to demonstrate to those in a world of sin and rebellion the benefits of living under God's perfect law and order. God will not stay His hand forever on the wickedness of this world. But in this final plan, He has given mankind one more chance. What will we do with it?

If we fail, it means the eventual death and destruction of mankind, and this earth along with him. Now, this doesn't necessarily mean God will destroy the earth with some cataclysmic catastrophe. On the contrary, if we continue to run this world as we have, paying no attention to how we are destroying our environment, having little or no regard for human life, and totally ignoring God and His law, then we ourselves will be agents of the earth's destruction.

Yet if we succeed, we will live forever and ever in the glory of the Lord. Then there will truly be final victory through Jesus Christ. So far only He has completely overcome sin and rebellion. Then He became sin for us and made it possible for us to live as He did. He left us the example of His sinless life and sent us the Holy Spirit to give us the power to complete the task that is now ours. He has given us the keys; now He waits for us to use them to destroy rebellion, evil, and sin…forever and ever.

Our Creed

The Cathedral of the Holy Spirit

I BELIEVE in the Father Almighty, who created the heavens and the earth.

I BELIEVE that God's original purpose was to create and maintain a universal community in which there would be creativity and productivity in an environment of health, peace, and harmony.

I BELIEVE in Jesus Christ, the only begotten Son of God the Father. I believe that Jesus was conceived of the Holy Ghost; born of the virgin Mary; died for the forgiveness of our sins, shedding His precious blood; was buried; and rose again on the third day. After His resurrection He preached the gospel of the Kingdom for 40 days and then ascended into Heaven, where He now sits at the right hand of God, the Father, interceding for the Church, His Bride.

I BELIEVE in the Holy Spirit, in His work on earth as Teacher, Comforter, and Guide. I believe in divine healing provided through the atoning blood of Jesus Christ. I believe in the Word of God and in the Living Word, Jesus Christ, Incarnate.

I BELIEVE that the Kingdom of God is built in trust and that the strategy of the Kingdom is love. I believe that God will destroy the destroyer of the earth. I believe in the holy universal Church built upon Jesus Christ, the Chief Cornerstone, the foundation being the Apostles and the Prophets.

I BELIEVE in the second coming of Jesus Christ, which will occur when the gospel of the Kingdom has been preached to all the earth as a witness. I believe that when Christ returns He will judge the quick and the dead and that He will establish God's Kingdom, of which there will be no end.

AND HE SHALL REIGN FOREVER AND EVER, HALLELUJAH!

Afterword

Pastor Don Paulk

We speak of the Kingdom. We talk of the establishment of the Kingdom. We talk of knowing the Kingdom, of accepting the Kingdom, and of receiving the Kingdom. Whatever terms we use, the important thing is that we *enter* the Kingdom. Yet, perhaps the first step should be understanding the Kingdom.

With our finite, mortal minds, it is impossible for us to know all the ways of God. But I fully believe that He has revealed enough of His Kingdom to us that we can indeed enter therein.

A few years ago I visited a few foreign countries. I spent a few days in Africa, a couple of days in Italy, and a few days in England. It was an enlightening experience.

Actually, I was not really prepared for the culture shock that I experienced. It all began at the airport in Lagos. Our little group had the only white faces in the entire international airport. I felt what it was like to really be in the minority! The waiters, waitresses, cab drivers, immigration authorities—everyone we had to deal with dealt with us as if we were aliens. That is exactly what we were in Lagos. I then understood what it felt like to be an alien in a country that was not mine.

There was one exception, however. When we entered Bishop Idahosa's church in Benin City, I felt completely at home. The faces there were of color also, but my pale face didn't seem to matter to them in the least. I was their brother because we were citizens of the same Kingdom. Being a citizen of the Kingdom of God transcends race, nationality, ethnic or cultural backgrounds, and economic, social, or educational differences. Children of God are all citizens of the same Kingdom.

When our group came to Rome, Italy, the people there treated us a little better, especially those who wanted our money. When they found out we were tourists, they were ready to do business with us. After we were sold a few donuts and some coffee at a sidewalk cafe for almost a hundred American dollars, it was not difficult to realize what kingdom they were interested in! They quickly realized that we were from another country. To them, we were aliens—and, to use an old Southern phrase, "easy pickin's."

London was a little more sophisticated, but even there I quickly realized that the original Picadilly was not the same as the local cafeteria of the same name here in my neighborhood. After all that traveling, I just wanted to get back to where I could get a foot-long hot dog at Zesto's.

Even as we travel to other countries and become aware of the differences in our various cultures, we must realize there are two other different cultures or kingdoms that exist. Let's call these two kingdoms the Kingdom of God or Light and the kingdom of satan or darkness. We all live in one or the other of these kingdoms. We are either citizens of the Kingdom of God or we are citizens of the kingdom of satan. We can, in fact, become comfortable in either one of those kingdoms and allow it to be our place of citizenship.

Our responsibility, then, is to determine which of these two kingdoms we want to belong to. When the two kingdoms are compared, we quickly see the vast differences. In the Kingdom of God there is peace, tranquility, love, harmony, joy, and fulfillment. In the kingdom of satan there is frustration, conflict, violence, greed, avarice, and jealousy. When we realize this, our choice becomes clear.

Subsequently, our task is not only to enter the Kingdom of God ourselves, but also to lead others into this Kingdom. One of the saddest indictments in Scripture is against those who will neither enter the Kingdom of God nor allow others to enter (see Mt. 23:13). When we enter the Kingdom of God, we must do everything within our power to convince others that the Kingdom of God is the Kingdom they should seek.

What is the Kingdom? It is not a fairy tale or some unreachable concept that we can never realize. To me, the Kingdom comes down to a life style—both a corporate life style for our society and a personal life style for us as individuals.

When we really enter the Kingdom ourselves, we will find it so exciting that we will be anxious to bring others in with us. Only those who have never really entered the Kingdom of God feel like an alien in it. When we are born into the Kingdom of God, we become full-fledged citizens of this new Kingdom and aliens to the kingdom of darkness, which is ruled by satan.

In our attempt to comprehend the Kingdom of God, we use several descriptive terms of what it is we are trying to do. Sometimes we say we are trying to "establish" the Kingdom. But that is not possible. Indeed, it is presumptuous for us to claim to do something as grand as that, for that is what God Himself has already done. God Himself has already firmly established His Kingdom.

When He established the universe, He ordained design and structure. When He created the earth and all that dwelt on it, again there was obvious structure and design. God then assigned man the responsibility of having dominion over what He had created here on earth.

We, then, have not established the Kingdom of God. God did it Himself. So what do we do? What is our relationship with the Kingdom of God?

Once we begin to understand God's intentions, then I think a better term is the one the wonderful late Ern Baxter used. He suggested that we "receive" the Kingdom. After all, the Kingdom is already intact, and God is sovereign. He doesn't need our vote of confidence to be King. We didn't elect Him God. Our role is to simply accept the fact that God has created every thing and has placed us to have dominion over His creation. What we then were created for is to understand, accept, and receive the Kingdom of God; enter it; and enjoy its benefits.

Is the Kingdom of God some new concept come to us by recent revelation? No, the Kingdom of God was established in the heart of God from the very foundation of the world. When Jesus came back to the earth for 40 days after He was crucified, He preached the message of the Kingdom of God.

The message of John the Baptist, on the other hand, was repentance. As the forerunner, he prepared the way for Jesus Christ. He cried out, "Prepare ye the way." He called for his hearers to repent and be baptized.

There are still those today who preach the message of John the Baptist: "Repent and be baptized!" But that isn't the message of the Kingdom of God. Jesus was the fulfillment of the message of the Kingdom. He went beyond repentance and salvation; He laid down a life style in His teachings.

So what is the difference between what we call the Kingdom message and the message of salvation? It is very simple. Metaphorically speaking, the message of salvation provides us with the ticket to ride the train when we arrive at the station. Without the ticket of salvation, we can't even board the "Kingdom train." Salvation is a prerequisite to the Kingdom.

Suppose you purchased a ticket to get on the Kingdom train, then stood around and watched other people board the train. You heard the conductor calling out, "All aboard," but you just stood idly by until the train pulled away from the station. You would have missed the Kingdom train.

The message of salvation is a transitional message. It gets you from one place to the other. It is the boot that kicks you out of the kingdom of satan and the key that opens the door to the Kingdom of God. The salvation message is absolutely necessary. But if we simply stop there, we will miss what Jesus was trying to tell us about His Kingdom.

The message of salvation convicts us of our sins. It shows us that we are sinners. It brings us to the realization that we are living in the wrong kingdom. It reveals to us that we are serving the wrong king; it makes us uncomfortable with the kingdom we are in. The salvation message makes us feel as if we are aliens, rather than citizens, of the kingdom of satan.

But we cannot stop there. If we walk up to the grand entrance of a castle and stand and admire it, but refuse to use the key that was placed in our hands, then we will never enter that castle nor enjoy its benefits. Similarly, we can receive salvation but never fully enter the Kingdom of God or enjoy all the benefits of the Kingdom that God prepared for us.

I fear that at times we make the Kingdom of God too inaccessible or too difficult for others to enter. First we remind them that we enter the Kingdom by violence and that it is taken by the violent. Then we tell them that the Kingdom is like a sword that separates families. Finally, we warn them that the Kingdom brings out evil spirits in people and throws us into tremendous spiritual warfare. All of these things may well be true. But my question is, why do we dwell on these aspects rather than on the many wonderful benefits of the Kingdom?

Certainly, there will always be conflicts in this life. There always will be conflict where satan is trying to protect his evil kingdom. But we must remember that the victory has already been won. God has already established His Kingdom. We only have to receive it.

Sometimes I talk with my wife Clariece and we commiserate about all the "spiritual warfare" that seems to have erupted because we preach the Kingdom message. I tell you truthfully, I have many mixed emotions about this whole concept. I sometimes tell her that if this tremendous warfare is all I can look forward to in the Kingdom of God, then I think I'll take my salvation ticket and wait for the next train!

The point is, I really believe we make it hard for people to enter the Kingdom of God because we dwell on and emphasize the great warfare that surrounds it. Then people say, "If that's what the Kingdom is all about, then I don't want any part of it. I have enough fighting in the kingdom I'm already in."

I repeat, I like to look at the Kingdom of God as a new life style. It is a life style that brings fulfillment and peace to our lives, not more conflict and warfare. There is enough of that in the kingdom of satan. When sharing the message of the Kingdom with others, then, we must remember there is no great incentive in leaving one battle just to join another one already in progress.

Neither does the message of the Kingdom involve mystical concepts never heard of before. On the contrary, the Kingdom is the principles that Jesus taught in the Sermon on the Mount in Matthew 5. It is the Beatitudes. It is living out the Golden Rule of treating other people as you wish to be treated. It is keeping the

Ten Commandments. It is caring for the widows and the orphans. It is caring for the environment God placed us in. It is doing away with prejudice. It is doing away with war and violence. It is being salt and light in a world of darkness.

God wants a Kingdom on earth that reflects the Kingdom that already exists in Heaven. It is a total change of life style. I think that's what people are really looking for. They may not understand all our religious jargon about "establishing" or "receiving" the Kingdom, but they know they are tired of living in darkness and conflict. They will welcome a change in life style if we convince them that the Kingdom of God brings what they are looking for.

Bishop Paulk once preached a sermon where he explained that Heaven is an extension of what we believe and practice here on earth. If we enter the Kingdom of God here, then we will merely extend our life style in an eternal dimension. But if we reside in the kingdom of darkness, we will continue that life style of hatred, violence, and conflict throughout eternity. It all begins right here. Therefore, entering the Kingdom of God means changing our life style to one that is compatible with the existence God has prepared for us eternally. Rather than living with hate, greed, avarice, jealousy, prejudice, violence, and crime, we begin to live in an attitude of love, mercy, compassion, forgiveness, sharing, giving, health, and happiness.

For example, I understand that my brother Earl has totally changed his life style concerning his eating habits. He tells me that he isn't eating any meat. Now if you would tell me that I've got to quit eating meat, I would go into a total panic! I don't think I can live without my red meat. But, from what I hear, it has not only been an easy transition for him, but a joyful one as well. He says he is feeling better than he has in years. In fact, he feels like a young man again. Now that gets my attention!

So it is with changing kingdoms. Sometimes we fear the unknown. Will we be able to do it? Will it be painful? Can we stand it? We want to stay where we are safe. We want to keep eating our hamburgers and french fries. We don't want to move into a new life style where we have to eat "veggies." But then, after we move into the Kingdom of God, the anticipated demons and all the terrible warfare we have been warned about just doesn't materialize. We can actually flourish in this new Kingdom!

If the message of the Kingdom of God is indeed God's true message, then not only will He make it endurable for us, but I believe He also will make it a glorious adventure. I don't believe the Kingdom of God will make martyrs of us. Whatever warfare we may encounter will get so lost in the glory of the Kingdom that it will be inconsequential.

I know there is a devil and that there are demons and evil spirits all about us. However, I've also found out that, for the most part, the devil is a blowhard. The Bible says we are not to "give place" to the devil (see Eph. 4:27). Do we realize how much of a place of prominence we give him when we attribute all this great warfare to him? He smugly grins and says, "I have them right where I want them. I'm really hurting them." I'm tired of giving satan that satisfaction.

A good friend and I were talking once and he asked me about my daddy. He had heard that my daddy wasn't afraid of dogs and wanted to know if the stories he had heard about my daddy's encounters with vicious dogs were true.

Let me give you a firsthand account. When I was a boy and got out of school in the afternoons, Mama often sent me with Daddy as he made his pastoral house calls.

On a number of occasions we would go to the house of someone who had a big, bad dog in their yard. Often there would be a sign in the yard: "Beware of Dog." I would watch Daddy walk up to the fence, open the gate, and walk straight into the yard with the dog growling, barking, and acting as if he were going to attack Daddy. Daddy would look the dog straight in the eye. If he said anything, he would say, "Get away from here, dog" or something like that. He never kicked at the dog. He never went out of his way to run at the dog, but he never took a step back from the dog or turned his back on the dog. He, for the most part, just totally ignored the dog, who would yap on harmlessly.

I recall one man, hearing his dog barking and growling, rushing outside to pull his huge bulldog off Daddy. But Daddy was smiling, standing on the porch, and the dog was in the yard growling. The man said, "Preacher, how did you do that? Don't you know that dog bites every person who dares to come inside this fence? You are the only person I've ever seen him let get in without biting them. How did you do it, Preacher?"

Daddy said, "Very simple. I just paid him no attention. He knows that I'm not afraid of him. He would attack me only if he thought I was afraid of him." I never saw my daddy get bitten by a dog.

I think demons are the same way. They like to growl and intimidate; they like to frighten us, roaring and flexing their muscles to get us to run scared. They also have great egos. They love to hear us talking about them and how they are surfacing and causing great warfare. As for me, I want to do like Daddy. I want to just stare them in the eye as if to say, "Eat dirt," then ignore them and get on with the business of the Kingdom. As long as satan can keep us at bay with his intimidating little demons, he will control our agenda.

The time has come for us to quit giving these demons notoriety. They have already been defeated. They are living on borrowed time. Why let them hinder us from doing what God has called us to do? We are called to receive and enter the Kingdom, then invite others to do the same.

In my simple mind the concept of the Kingdom is indeed simple. I don't want to complicate it. So let's try not to make it hard for others to enter the Kingdom. If you must warn them about all the devils and demons that are surfacing, then also tell them the good news. Tell them about all the guardian angels God has released to protect us. Tell them how a few angels can put thousands of demons to flight. Remind them that "He who is in you is greater than he who is in the world" (1 Jn. 4:4b).

You see, I really want to live in the Kingdom. I want to be a citizen of the Kingdom of God. I want to live by its principles. But I don't want to have to build a moat around it and stand guard every night to keep from being overrun by the demons. I want to enjoy its wonderful benefits.

Let's make the Kingdom of God easy for people to enter. Let's make it as attractive and inviting as possible. Let's make people want to run to the Kingdom of God rather than run away in fear because of the great warfare. Let's allow them to see the benefits of love and joy and all the wonderful attributes in our own lives that are inherent in the Kingdom of God.

In short, you are living either in the kingdom of darkness or in the Kingdom of God. If you have been saved, you have been extended an invitation to become a citizen in the Kingdom of God. The Kingdom of God is not a place to dread because of all the warfare that surrounds it. Nor is it a place to be frightened away from by the demons. It is a place of joy, contentment, love, harmony, and peace. It is the Kingdom that God has prepared for all who love Him and who await His appearing. So don't be left at the depot. Get your ticket of salvation ready. The Kingdom train is building up its steam and preparing to pull away from the station. Don't be left standing. The conductor is already calling, "All aboard! All aboard..."